Faith Under Fire

David Faust

STANDARD
PUBLISHING
Cincinnati, Ohio

Library of Congress Cataloging-in Publication Data

Faust, David, 1954-
    Faith under fire / transforming power from 1 and 2 Peter / David Faust
        p. cm.
    Includes bibliographical references
    ISBN 0-7847-0637-9
    1. Bible. N.T. Peter—Devotional literature. I. Title
BS 2795.4.F38 1997
227'.9206--dc21   97-9226
                                                CIP

Edited by Theresa C. Hayes
Cover design by Schultz/Ward

The Standard Publishing Company, Cincinnati, Ohio.
A division of Standex International Corporation.

04 03 02 01 00 99 98 97   5 4 3 2 1

To Charles and Penny Faust,
who demonstrate that
the best way to keep the faith
is to keep giving it away.

Contents

Lighting the First Spark

"Y ou *will* get wet on this ride. You may get *very* wet."
Have you ever noticed a sign like that while standing in line
at an amusement park? You can hear people scream as water
shoots across their raft or log flume. Drenched, happy riders—with T-
shirts soaked, shoes full of water, hair and eyeglasses dripping—slog
past the folk still waiting in line. Strangely enough, despite the screams
and wet clothes, everyone is usually laughing. Stranger still, you and I
stay in line for the ride so the same thing can happen to us!

"You *will* get wet on this ride"? Yes, that's exactly what you want to
do. It's why you came to the park in the first place—to experience the
adventure of an exciting, refreshing ride across the rapids. There's
something about the ride's air of "danger" that appeals to your sense
of daring.

But let's be honest. The "danger" of an amusement park ride really
represents nothing but a relatively low-risk quest for entertainment—
it's little more than a short-lived diversion. A day at a high-priced modern amusement park is mainly just hazardous to your wallet!

If you're looking for genuine adventure, don't settle for feeble imita-
tions. Jesus calls us to something far more worthwhile than the world's
cheap thrills. Get close to Jesus Christ, and you'll find yourself faced
with a life-changing, future-altering, hope-kindling, adventure of faith.

That's what happened to Simon Peter. When he met Jesus, it was
like a piece of hard flint striking against a stone. Sparks—good
sparks—began to fly. The flame of faith in Peter's heart grew hotter and

purer with every lesson he learned and every trial he faced.

It all started with a simple but profound invitation the Lord extended one day by the Sea of Galilee. Jesus told Peter and his brother Andrew, "Come, follow me, and I will make you fishers of men" (Mark 1:17). Did Peter realize what lay ahead? Probably not. Did he foresee how Jesus would challenge and change his preconceived ideas about the Messiah? Did he picture himself walking on water, gathering up a basketful of miraculous bread and fish, or traveling as a missionary far beyond the borders of his homeland? Did he ever expect to dine in the home of a Gentile like Cornelius? Could he imagine the way his faith would come under fire again and again? Did he anticipate that terrible night of Jesus' arrest when he would deny his Lord three times?

Go ahead, Peter. Follow Jesus. But be warned: You're going to get wet! And this is going to be no frivolous amusement park ride, but a life-endangering choice to fully live for Christ.

How do you picture Simon Peter? Many not-so-flattering adjectives come to mind when we think of him. Brash. Impulsive. Impatient. Quick to speak, quick to act.

But there's a lot to admire—and perhaps, a lot of *ourselves*—in this humble fisherman. Despite Peter's flaws, the Lord transformed him into a courageous, effective leader whose faith shines from the pages of Scripture like gold refined by fire.

Next to the apostle Paul, Scripture mentions Peter more than any other apostle. He was with Jesus throughout the Lord's public ministry. They were together in glorious places like the mount of transfiguration, and in painful places like the Garden of Gethsemane. Peter was there at Jesus' empty tomb, and in the upper room when the resurrected Christ showed the disciples his hands and feet.

Peter was God's messenger who used the "keys of the kingdom" when he proclaimed the gospel both to the Jews (on the Day of Pentecost) and to the Gentiles (at the home of Cornelius). God also led Peter to write two short, encouraging books filled with hope for suffering Christians.

It isn't easy to follow Jesus today. It wasn't easy to follow Jesus in the first century, either. Then and now, faith comes under fire from many directions. Make no mistake about it: the Christian life isn't just a casual ride in the park. You're going to get wet on this ride! Serving Christ is no trivial, fun-filled diversion. Living by faith is a high-risk endeavor—not for the faint of heart. But through all the hardships, like Peter, you'll have the time of your life as you experience the adventure of serving the King of kings.

As we study Peter's inspired letters (1 and 2 Peter), we can see how God shaped a rough Galilean fisherman into a great leader. We will discover new insights that can spark fresh bursts of spiritual growth. Or perhaps we will simply rediscover the old familiar truths we need to rekindle some dying embers of faith.

Through it all, we can find encouragement to continue in our walk with God—even when our faith is under fire.

CHAPTER ONE

Let Go of the Net

1 Peter 1:1, 2; Luke 5:1-11

Several years ago, my family vacationed at a campground in Ontario. We stayed in a rustic cabin in the woods, next to the St. Lawrence River. Several members of our extended family shared the campsite, including my three brothers-in-law. Nearly every day for two weeks, we rose early in the morning to go fishing. Now, you must understand, none of us are skillful sailors or fishermen. Our early morning fishing expeditions were more about spending time with the other guys than catching fish. Each morning we met by the dock around five, rowed out to the middle of the river, tossed our lines into the water, and watched the sun rise. After a couple of leisurely hours, we'd row back to shore, devour a hearty pancake breakfast, and brag about the size of the fish we almost caught.

One cold morning, I felt sleepier than usual as I crawled out of my warm bed and walked to the dock through the early-morning mist. My sleepy mind was in a fog too. I climbed into a rowboat with my brother-in-law, Tom, and grabbed the oars. With my back to the dock, I began to row—but the boat refused to move. For a moment I wondered why the current was so exceptionally strong that day. But within a few seconds I recognized the real problem: our boat was still tied to the dock! To make matters worse, by the time we realized what was wrong and loosened the ropes, the guys in the other boat noticed our predicament and began laughing at us. Through the years, my brothers-in-law often have enjoyed reminding me about the time I tried to row a boat while it was tied to a dock.

Do you ever feel like you're rowing a boat that's going nowhere? Do you sometimes find yourself trying hard, but despite your best efforts, things don't turn out the way you hoped? You're straining and pulling with all your strength, but making little progress? What is holding you back? What ropes are tying you to the dock?

One day Jesus sat in Peter's fishing boat while the fishermen washed their nets nearby. At Jesus' request, Peter pushed the boat a few feet from shore so the Lord could speak without being crushed by the crowd. (No doubt the flat surface of the lake also amplified Jesus' voice—a natural sound system long before microphones and public address systems.)

Can you picture the scene? The water lapped gently at the sides of the boat, as a great crowd of listeners stood on the sandy shore or sat on the docks listening as Jesus taught the Word of God. Surely no one listened more closely than the fiery fisherman who shared the boat with Jesus that day. Perhaps Peter began to realize: someday he'd have to let go of his fishing net, and for that matter, let go of anything else that held him back from following Jesus.

UNTANGLING PETER'S PERSONALITY

HIS NAME

Peter's parents called him Simon, from the Hebrew *shama*, "to hear." Simon was a common name among the Jews because it is derived from "Simeon," the name of one of the sons of Jacob (and one of the twelve tribes of Israel).

"Peter" comes from the Greek *petros*, which means a rock. Though he himself was not very rocklike at times, Peter was "the rock man" because he was so loyal to Jesus, the rock of our salvation. Jesus nick-named Simon "Cephas," which is Aramaic for "rock" (John 1:42), and the apostle Paul liked to use this name for Peter (1 Corinthians 1:12; 9:5). Scripture assigns Peter several other descriptive titles as well: "pillar of the church" (Galatians 2:9), "apostle" (1 Peter 1:1), "fellow elder," and "witness of Christ's suffering" (1 Peter 5:1).

HIS FAMILY

Scripture tells us nothing about Peter's parents except his father's name. Jesus referred to Peter as "Simon son of Jonah (or John)" (Matthew 16:17; John 1:42). Peter's brother, Andrew, first introduced him to Jesus (John 1:40-42). Evidently Peter and his brother grew up in the town of Bethsaida, then later lived in a house in the neighboring city of Capernaum (Matthew 8:5, 14).

Though we do not know his spouse's name, 1 Corinthians 9.5 makes it clear that Peter had a wife who accompanied him on his preaching journeys. (One has to wonder what was it like to be *Mrs.* Simon Peter?) Peter's mother-in-law is mentioned in Matthew 8:14 and Mark 1:29-31, which describe how Jesus healed her fever.

HIS OCCUPATION

Some of the best-known Bible stories about Peter have to do with his work as a fisherman. Twice Jesus amazed Peter with a miraculous catch of fish (Luke 5:1-11; John 21:1-14). Another time, when Peter followed Jesus' instructions and threw his line into the lake, he caught a fish with a four-drachma coin in its mouth—exactly the amount needed to pay the temple tax or tribute money (Matthew 17:24-27).

My mental image of Peter includes wind-blown hair and chapped skin from many chilly nights at sea, and hands callused from handling ropes, nets, and oars. His personality comes into sharper focus when I imagine the smell of fish, the sound of Peter's voice calling instructions to his brother about where to drop their nets, and the sight of Peter bargaining with potential customers to get a fair price for his catch.

HIS ETHNIC BACKGROUND

Peter was saturated in Jewish culture, and no doubt grew up familiar with the Hebrew Bible. Every chapter of 1 Peter contains at least one quotation from the Old Testament. In fact, although 1 Peter is a relatively short epistle, it quotes from all three major sections of the Hebrew Scriptures: the Law, the Prophets, and the Psalms.

Peter's Jewish world view made it difficult for him to accept Gentiles as full brothers and sisters in Christ. He must have been quite shocked when God sent him to preach to Cornelius (Acts 10:9-35). Years later, Peter still struggled to act lovingly toward non-Jewish people (see Galatians 2:11-14). Understanding his background makes Peter's reference to his multiethnic readers, both Jews and Gentiles, as "a chosen people, a royal priesthood, a holy nation, a people belonging to God" (1 Peter 2:9) even more significant.

HIS COMPANIONS

Peter was not a lone ranger. He had several good friends and coworkers, some of whom were also associated with the apostle Paul. Silas (or Silvanus), mentioned in 1 Peter 5:12, was either Peter's scribe who wrote down the letter, or the one who carried the letter to the churches. Evidently this was the same Silas who accompanied Paul on his second missionary journey (Acts 15:40).

Peter also speaks of "my son Mark" (1 Peter 5:13). Apparently this was the same Mark who accompanied Paul on his first missionary journey and who authored the second book of the New Testament. Peter's fond words for Mark as a spiritual "son" lead many Bible students to theorize that these two shared a special friendship, and that perhaps Mark's Gospel in some ways reflects the preaching and influence of Peter. While we can't be sure about that connection, we do know that when Peter was miraculously freed from prison, he immediately went to a prayer meeting at the home of Mary, Mark's mother (Acts 12:12).

HIS DISPOSITION

Three characteristics of Peter's personality seem to stand out in the Gospels.

He was quick to speak. It was Peter who spoke assertively for the rest of the apostles and confessed his faith in Christ; however, soon afterward Peter was the one who dared to rebuke Jesus when the Lord predicted his suffering and death as the Messiah (Matthew 16:13-24).

He was quick to act. Peter was a man of action—bold, impulsive, unafraid to take risks. He was the one who eagerly stepped out of the boat and walked on the water to Jesus (Matthew 14:29). He was the

one who tried to defend Jesus in the Garden of Gethsemane; he drew
his sword and cut off the ear of the high priest's servant (John 18:10).

He loved Jesus. Often we're too quick to criticize Peter's impetuous
ways. Yes, there were many rough spots in his personality. (Who
doesn't have some?) Yes, he sometimes struggled with anger and
impatience. (Who doesn't?) But even in his awkward moments, Peter
showed an intense love and loyalty for Jesus. Even on that bitter night
when he denied Jesus three times (Matthew 26:69-75), Peter's remorse
was deep precisely because his love for Jesus was deep.

HIS ROLE IN THE CHURCH

Peter overcame his weaknesses and failures to become one of the
best-known figures in all the Bible. New Testament writers mentioned
his name 210 times. Along with James and John, he was one of Jesus'
so-called "inner circle" who were with Jesus during private moments
like the transfiguration and the raising of Jairus' daughter (Luke 8:51;
9:28). In the four lists of apostles found in the New Testament, Peter's
name is recorded first each time (Matthew 10:2-4; Mark 3:16-19;
Luke 6:14-16; Acts 1:13), and he was a prominent leader throughout
the early days of the church recorded in the first half of the book of
Acts.

Peter was not concerned about making a name for himself, however.
His goal was to make known the name of Jesus Christ. Peter may have
been prominent, but nowhere does Scripture call him a pope or
require that others treat Peter with special honors. On the contrary,
when Cornelius fell in reverence at Peter's feet, Peter humbly told him
not to do it. "Stand up," he said, "I am only a man myself" (Acts
10:26).

Like a tangled fishnet, Peter's personality was somewhat complicated.
But the Lord gradually shaped Peter's character until he became a
dynamic fisher of men.

Peter was a diamond in the rough whom the Lord polished into a
beautiful gem. If the Lord can do that for someone like Peter, he can
do it for us also.

UNTANGLING 1 AND 2 PETER

Peter's letters are part of a group of New Testament books known as
"general epistles" because, rather than being addressed to one particular city or individual, they were intended for general circulation among
the churches.[1] These books have also been termed "catholic epistles,"
since "catholic" means universal or worldwide. Yet another term that
fits Peter's letters is "encyclical," for these epistles were widely circulat-
ed as they passed from one church to another.

Peter does not call his readers by name, but mentions several important facts about them. They were *set apart*, "chosen according to the
foreknowledge of God" (1 Peter 1:1, 2). God's calling does not elimi-
nate personal responsibility; believers willingly choose to follow the
Lord. But Christians are indeed a "chosen people," set apart to enjoy
special privileges and to perform special services (1 Peter 2:9).

Peter also refers to his readers as *strangers* in the world. The Greek
word *parepidemos* means one who is an alien, an exile, a sojourner—a
displaced person or resident alien (compare Hebrews 11:13; 1 Peter
2:11). Since a Christian's highest citizenship is in Heaven, we are
always strangers here on earth. As someone has said, "This world is a
bridge. A wise man will pass over it, but will not build his house
upon it."

Furthermore, Peter's readers were *scattered*. They lived in various sections of the Roman province of Asia (modern-day Turkey). In 1 Peter
1:1, Peter uses the Greek word *diasporas* to describe the way the
Christians were dispersed or scattered, like grains of salt released from
the saltshaker to spread their savory influence on everything they
touch.[2]

First Peter 1:1 mentions most of the major provinces of first-century
Asia Minor. *Pontus* was the homeland of Aquila, the dedicated
Christian who made tents and served Christ alongside his wife Priscilla
and the apostle Paul (Acts 18:2). *Galatia, Cappadocia, Asia,* and *Bithynia*
are mentioned elsewhere in the New Testament (Acts 2:9; 16:7; 19:10;
Galatians 1:2). A look at a map of the region suggests the possibility
that Peter listed the provinces in order of the mail route followed by

Silvanus or whoever carried the letter from place to place. This enabled Peter's letters to be read and copied down in all the major cities and outlying towns.[3]

Peter's purpose for writing was clear. Earlier Jesus told him, "Strengthen your brothers" and "Feed my sheep" (Luke 22:32; John 21:17). In obedience to Jesus' command, Peter wrote 1 Peter to offer words of strength and spiritual nourishment to Christians who were suffering. There is a warm pastoral tone to Peter's words, especially in 1 Peter. William Barclay called 1 Peter "the lovely letter," and wrote that there has never been "any doubt about its charm."[4] Peter's goal in writing was to encourage his readers and testify that "this is the true grace of God. Stand fast in it" (1 Peter 5:12).

UNTANGLING THE COMMITMENT
JESUS REQUIRES

First Peter 1:2 mentions all three persons of the Trinity—or Godhead —the foreknowledge of the Father, the sanctifying work of the Spirit, and obedience to Jesus Christ.

Notice Peter's emphasis on obedience to Christ. Peter wanted his readers to follow Christ with the same kind of unfettered commitment Peter himself learned on the shore of the Sea of Galilee.

According to Luke 5:1-11, when Jesus finished teaching from Peter's boat, he instructed Peter, "Put out into deep water, and let down the nets for a catch." This was a difficult command. There were many reasons Peter could have refused Jesus' instruction.

For one thing, *Peter was tired*. He had just finished working the night shift. When Jesus first arrived on the scene, the fishermen were washing their nets (Luke 5:2). They were rinsing out the seaweed—which was all they had caught that night. In those days, fishermen would clear the debris out of their nets, mend any torn spots in the netting, then fold the nets and hang them on the docks or across the sail rigging to dry. Weary from a long, unproductive night, Peter probably was ready to go home and crawl into a warm bed.

Peter also was frustrated. He and his helpers had fished all night but caught nothing. Why should he drag his nets back out and try again? As someone quipped, "I never get frustrated; the reason is, to wit—If at first I don't succeed . . . I quit!" Sometimes it's hard to let go of past failures and try again.

Even more, Jesus' words *went against Peter's natural instincts.* He was a knowledgeable, experienced fisherman, and Jesus was asking him to do something that went directly against his well-honed instincts developed during years of sailing the Sea of Galilee. Put out into deep water? "No, Lord, the fish usually are easier to catch in the shallower water near the shore." Go fishing under the heat of the sun? "I don't think so, Lord; we catch more fish in the cool hours of the evening."

Can you picture Peter, and perhaps Andrew, James, and John, standing on the dock with their arms folded, pondering Jesus' strange request? Were there several other cynical fishermen in the crowd, ready to laugh at Peter if he actually went back out to sea? It was hard enough to catch fish under ideal conditions. Why do it Jesus' way?

Perhaps Peter was tempted to think, "Jesus, you were trained as a carpenter. But I'm the expert when it comes to fishing." Or, "Lord, you're a great teacher, and those parables you tell are very interesting. But what do you really know about my day-to-day world of catching fish?" If there was one area in Peter's life where he must have felt competent—one area where he might realistically say, "I don't need the Lord's help," it was fishing.

Nevertheless, *Peter was willing to obey.* He offered a mild objection: "Master, we've worked hard all night and haven't caught anything." But then Peter continued, "But because you say so, I will let down the nets."

What a great attitude! Put yourself in Peter's shoes. If the Lord asked you to do something that seemed unreasonable—perhaps even a bit ridiculous—would you do it "just because the Lord says so"?

When Peter called Jesus "master," he used an unusual word (*epistates*) which the Greeks used to describe the conductor of a musical orchestra, the coach of an athletic team, or the captain of a ship. It's as if Peter were saying, "Aye, aye, Captain! I may know a lot about fishing, but Jesus, you are in charge. You are the skipper of my boat and the Lord of my life!"

So with their breakfastless stomachs growling, sleepy from the unproductive night just past, perhaps ignoring the sarcastic guffaws of the watching crowd, Peter and his helpers rowed out to the deep water. They dropped their freshly cleansed nets and "caught such a large number of fish that their nets began to break" (Luke 5:6).

Jesus blesses his followers when, like Peter, we dare to let go of the "nets" of human wisdom that hold us back from trusting him. He wants us to say, "I'm weary, but *because you say so,* I will launch out again. I've tried and failed in the past, but *because you say so,* I will try again. The circumstances don't seem favorable, and it's hard to understand how you will help me in this situation, Lord. But I will launch out—even into the deep water and the risky areas—just *because you say so.*"

What was the result of Peter's obedience? His boat was filled with fish. Another boat was filled too. In fact, both boats were so heavy with fish they began to sink—and the disciples reacted with astonishment. Peter fell at Jesus' knees and exclaimed, "Go away from me, Lord; I am a sinful man!"

Now, this wasn't the first time Jesus had performed a miracle. He had already changed water into wine, cast out evil spirits, and healed many people, including Peter's own mother-in-law (see Luke 4:35-41). But this time, the Lord's miraculous power was displayed right in the center of Peter's everyday world—right in the fishing boat where he lived and worked.

Why did Peter call himself "a sinful man"? When he beheld the power and wisdom of Jesus, he saw his own weaknesses and imperfections more clearly. He was sorry for any subtle doubt that had been in his heart before, and for the "nets" of hesitation and unbelief that had held him back. Now it was time to make a full commitment. It was time to let go of the nets and cling to Jesus.

Jesus reassured Peter: "Don't be afraid; from now on you will catch men." Peter and the other disciples pulled their boats onto the shore, then "left everything"—the nets, the fish, everything!—and followed him (Luke 5:10, 11).

When we become aware of our guilt, our first reaction might be to pull away from the Lord in shame. But the best place for a sinner to be is right where Peter was: as close as possible to the Lord, kneeling in reverence before the Lord.

We're called to "obedience to Jesus Christ" (1 Peter 1:2). In your personal life, what is the Lord asking you to do? What is holding you back? Fear? Guilt? Hesitation? Lack of faith?

Is sin, like a tangled fishnet, hindering your walk with the Lord? If the Lord can turn a man like Peter into a great leader, surely there's hope for you and me.

Let go of the net.

NOTES: CHAPTER ONE

1. Other "general epistles" include James, Jude, and the three epistles of John. Some Bible students also include Hebrews in this category.

2. Acts 8:4 uses the verb form of *diasporas* when it says, "Those who had been *scattered* preached the word wherever they went."

3. See Wayne Grudem, *1 Peter* (Grand Rapids: Eerdmans, 1988), pp. 37, 38.

4. William Barclay, *The Letters of James and Peter* (Philadelphia: Westminster Press, 1976), p. 138.

CHAPTER TWO

When the Fire Hits Home

1 Peter 1:3-12; Matthew 16:21-28

F ire is one of the most terrifying words in the English language. We warn young children, "Don't play with fire." Our communities employ fire departments to prevent property damage and loss of life.

Fire finds its way into unpleasant metaphors. If you lack self-control, you have a "fiery" temper. When you're pressured at work, you feel like you're "on the firing line." If you lose your job, you get "fired." Jesus spoke of hell as a place where "the fire is not quenched" (Mark 9:48).

In 1988, a forest fire raged across 1.4 million acres of timberland in and around Wyoming's Yellowstone National Park. Sparked by a combination of lightning and human negligence, flames fanned by gusty winds roared through the underbrush, consuming everything in their path. Clouds of smoke billowed more than 25,000 feet into the air. Today, visitors still can see the results of the fiery devastation where acres of proud forest succumbed to the flames, mere kindling in nature's fireplace.

Hiking trails still meander through many of the burned-out parts of Yellowstone; but if you walk there, be prepared for some melancholy feelings. An eerie sense of loss whistles through the charred pine trees that jut from the soil like used matches in an enormous matchbook. Other trees—that grew tall and green for two hundred years or more— now lie blackened and scattered on the ground, fallen warriors in a swift but decisive battle with the flames. Few things on earth can withstand the fury of fire.

Oddly, though, as the forest rangers at Yellowstone will tell you, there actually can be a positive side to a forest fire. New populations of birds and insects thrive in the ruins. Ashes enrich the soil. The cones of some varieties of lodgepole pine trees do not open until they are seared by fire. Heat from a forest fire forces the pine cones to open, and young trees that sprout from the seeds will form a new forest a hundred years from now. In time, new life will spring from the acres of ashes.

Fire isn't all bad. It can destroy, but it also can cook your food and warm your house. It can purify, refine, and cleanse. Fire can symbolize pleasant emotions. A glowing candle represents the joy of a birthday, the solemnity of a wedding, or the quiet reverence of a Christmas Eve service. An enthusiastic football team is "fired up." Eager young Christians are "on fire for the Lord."

Jeremiah described God's word as a fire in his bones that he could not hold in (Jeremiah 20:9). John the Baptist foretold how the Messiah would baptize "with the Holy Spirit and with fire" (Matthew 3:11). On the Day of Pentecost, the Holy Spirit came upon the apostles like tongues of fire (Acts 2:3). "Do not put out the Spirit's fire," wrote the apostle Paul (1 Thessalonians 5:19).

The apostle Peter wrote his epistles to encourage Christians whose faith is under fire. Several years earlier, Jesus had helped Peter learn how the fiery trials of hardship can refine and purify a person's character.

THE FIRE OF SELF-SACRIFICE

One day Jesus asked his disciples, "Who do people say the Son of Man is?" Peter's response still rings true today: "You are the Christ, the Son of the living God" (Matthew 16:13-16). Jesus commended Peter for expressing this God-given insight. However, Peter and the other disciples did not yet understand very well what it *meant* for Jesus to be the Christ, or Messiah. They still assumed the Lord's messianic work mainly meant the establishment of a glorious earthly kingdom for the Jews, freedom from the domination of Rome, and prestigious positions for Jesus' followers.

But Jesus had something else in mind.

A PAINFUL PREDICTION

"From that time on Jesus began to explain to his disciples that he must go to Jerusalem and suffer many things at the hands of the elders, chief priests and teachers of the law, and that he must be killed and on the third day be raised to life" (Matthew 16:21).

He must suffer? He must be handed over to his enemies? He must be killed? These weren't the kinds of things the disciples looked for in a messiah. Jesus realized he would have to pass through the fire of suffering to accomplish his goal of saving sinners, but he still needed to teach his disciples these difficult truths. This was hard for Peter to accept. Interrupting Jesus' lesson, Peter pulled Jesus to the side where they could speak privately and began to rebuke the Lord: "Never, Lord! This shall never happen to you!" (see Matthew 16:22). I marvel at Peter's audacity! How could he contradict Jesus and rebuke the Son of God, as if he knew better than the Lord himself did? Yet it's probably wise for each of us to ask, Do I ever find *myself* questioning the Lord, as if my knowledge were superior to his?

Earlier, Jesus responded to Peter's confession of faith with warm words of blessing. But this time, he met Peter's rebuke with some stinging words of his own: "Get behind me, Satan! You are a stumbling block to me; you do not have in mind the things of God, but the things of men" (Matthew 16:23).

Peter's ideas about God's will needed to pass through the refining fire of God's wisdom. Peter had adopted the common sense human point of view that says, "Avoid suffering at all costs." But God's point of view is, "Sometimes suffering is the road to glory." Human wisdom says, "Give me a crown, not a cross." But God's way says, "The cross comes before the crown." Human wisdom says, "The message of the cross is foolishness." But Heaven's wisdom says, "The message of the cross . . . is the power of God" (1 Corinthians 1:18).

A PRICE TO PAY

The death and resurrection of Christ form the very crux—the central truth—of the Christian faith (compare 1 Corinthians 15:1-4). Our word "crux" comes from the Latin word for "cross" (*cruc*) as does our word "crucial." Jesus' death on the cross was crucial—the heart of all we believe.

Our sin required the cross, for we cannot be right with God through our own human efforts (Romans 3:23; James 2:10). God's holiness required the cross, for only through Christ's sacrifice could God uphold his justice by punishing sin, and at the same time demonstrate his grace by forgiving sin (Romans 3:26).[1] The Scriptures required the cross, for Isaiah 53:4-6 predicted the Messiah's suffering.

Yet, like Peter, we recoil at the thought of the cross. Peter loved Jesus. He did not want to see his Lord endure the fiery trial of crucifixion. But what the Lord said next probably stunned Peter even more: "If anyone would come after me, he must deny himself and take up his cross and follow me. For whoever wants to save his life will lose it, but whoever loses his life for me will find it" (Matthew 16:24, 25).

Could Jesus really be saying that the fiery trial of crucifixion is ours to taste too? When Jesus died on the cross, he paid the price for our salvation once and for all (Hebrews 10:10-12). We cannot earn or deserve eternal life, nor can our personal suffering somehow win God's favor. But, make no mistake about it, there is a price to be paid in personal discipleship. In a wonderful paradox, Christ asks us to give up our lives, then find them again.

A PRICELESS PROFIT

Jesus asked, "What good will it be for a man if he gains the whole world, yet forfeits his soul?" (Matthew 16:26). We could also look at Jesus' question from the other direction. The flip side is, "Why worry about losing the whole world, as long as your soul is secure in Christ?"

Perhaps questions like these raced through Peter's mind as he began to write his first epistle. His first-century readers had given up a lot to follow Christ. But in the process they found the priceless profit of eternal life. Eager words poured from the apostle's pen, as Peter introduced the exciting theme of a Christian's "living hope." Apparently, he could hardly contain his enthusiasm: in the original Greek, 1 Peter 1:3-9 consists of one long run-on sentence! Our English versions break the thoughts into separate sentences, but we can still sense Peter's excitement when he wrote, "Praise be to the God and Father of our Lord Jesus Christ! In his great mercy he has given us new birth into a living hope" (1 Peter 1:3).

People hungered for hope in the first century. We still do today. Biblical hope is patient optimism—a confident expectation rooted in the steadfast promises of God. A hopeful person can say, "In the *present*, I'm confident about the *future*, because of what God has done in the *past*."

Peter says we have a "*living* hope." Like most living things, our hope is dynamic, vital, growing—an attitude by which we live. Christians agree with the psalmist who prayed, "But as for me, I will always have hope; I will praise you more and more" (Psalm 71:14). Our hope is "living" because *Jesus* is alive. As an old hymn says, "I serve a risen Savior, He's in the world today." We have hope, Peter insists, through "the resurrection of Jesus Christ from the dead" (1 Peter 1:3).

Furthermore, Christians will receive the priceless profit of "an inheritance that can never perish, spoil or fade" (v. 4). It's hard to find anything in this world that never perishes, spoils, or fades. Do you own any valuables that have faded with age? In my office I keep a photograph of my wife. The picture was taken on our wedding day twenty-two years ago. I can assure you, my wife's beauty has not faded, but the photo has begun to lose its sharpness and color. In Washington, DC, important documents like the Declaration of Independence and the Constitution are kept in glass cases away from damaging pollution and excess light, yet they still fade as time passes. Our priceless salvation, though, is unfading.

In Old Testament times, people looked forward to receiving a physical inheritance in the land of Canaan, but that inheritance was defiled and ruined by sin (see Leviticus 18:24-28). By contrast, our spiritual inheritance never will be defiled. Heaven never will lose its luster. The Bible uses the bright unfading colors of precious stones to help us picture the brilliance of Heaven's glory (Revelation 21:11-21).

Until we enter Heaven, through faith we are "shielded by God's power" (1 Peter 1:5). Here Peter uses a Greek military term (*phroureo*) for shielding, guarding, or protecting. In 2 Corinthians 11:32, Paul used the word to describe the way the king of Damascus had his soldiers guard the city to keep Paul from escaping. In Philippians 4:7, Paul used the same term to assure us that the peace of God "will *guard* your hearts and minds in Christ Jesus."

Wouldn't you feel safe if you had your own personal security guard? During my ministry with a church in New York, I sometimes visited patients at a hospital in a dangerous part of the city. When a young woman from out of town was admitted for surgery, my wife Candy and I decided to assist her family by preparing them a homemade meal. Candy prepared a delicious-looking lasagna and a loaf of homemade bread, and arranged the food in a large picnic basket. After driving my car to the hospital, I found a parking space on a busy street, and set out on foot with the picnic basket—looking and feeling a bit like Little Red Riding Hood! No one bothered me as I walked through the crime-ridden neighborhood. But the next time I visited the hospital, I took along my friend Tony, who was a detective for the New York City transit police. I felt a lot safer with a personal bodyguard along.

The church has a bodyguard. The Lord Jesus himself guards and protects the church, which is his body. He shields and protects us by his power as long as we cling to him by faith.

THE FIRE OF TESTING

God does not promise us trouble-free lives, however. As Job's friend Eliphaz commented, "Man is born to trouble as surely as sparks fly upward" (Job 5:7). Every trial is a spark that threatens to put our faith under fire.

THE KINDS OF TRIALS WE FACE

Trials come in many different forms. Peter writes, "you may have had to suffer grief in all kinds of trials" (1 Peter 1:6). "All kinds" translates the Greek word *poikilos,* which means varied, many-faceted, manifold, or multicolored. Hardships are many-faceted. They come in various shades.

Some folk live with chronic physical pain. Others suffer from unrelenting bouts of depression. Still others suffer daily from broken friendships, failed marriages, defiant children, or stressful pressures at work. Never assume others have easy lives. Some trials are just more visible than others.

It's encouraging to realize, however, that Peter uses a form of the same word (*poikiles*) in 1 Peter 4:10 in reference to "God's grace in its various forms." Yes, trials come in various forms, but God's grace comes in many different forms too. His grace is sufficient for every hardship.

Peter's original readers faced a particularly painful kind of trial. The Emperor Nero, who ruled Rome from A.D. 54 to 68, initiated a brief but savage persecution against Christians during the latter part of his reign. According to the Roman historian Tacitus, rumors spread that Nero himself had ordered the burning of Rome in July, A.D. 64. Nero attempted to divert the charge by blaming the Christians instead. Tacitus recorded that the Christians were mocked and subjected to cruel torture: "Covered with the skins of beasts, they were torn by dogs and perished, or were nailed to crosses, or were doomed to the flames and burned, to serve as a nightly illumination when daylight had expired. Nero offered his gardens for the spectacle . . . ."[2] Though Peter's first-century readers lived in the outlying provinces rather than the capital city, they lived under the shadow of persecution nonetheless, and no doubt heard reports of the fiery trials afflicting their Christian friends in Rome.

THE DURATION OF OUR TRIALS

Peter offers reassurance, however, with the simple phrase, "for a little while" (1 Peter 1:6). Our trials on earth are short in comparison to eternity. Even a lifetime of suffering lasts only "a little while," but Heaven lasts forever.

During my ten-year ministry in New York, the church endured a particularly difficult year. We were outgrowing our inadequate facilities, but lacked the finances to expand; a hurricane swamped our church lawn and knocked out power for several days; a burglar broke into my house; my car was badly damaged by vandals; and to top things off, a small earthquake shook our community early one Saturday morning. The day after the earthquake, I told the congregation, "This year my house has been burglarized, my car has been vandalized, my church has been traumatized, and my neighborhood has been tremorized . . . *but my faith is still energized!*" Temporary troubles help us appreciate the permanency of God.

The apostle Paul said it this way: "Therefore we do not lose heart. Though outwardly we are wasting away, yet inwardly we are being renewed day by day. For our light and momentary troubles are achieving for us an eternal glory that far outweighs them all" (2 Corinthians 4:16, 17). To put this into perspective, in the same letter Paul details some of his problems. He endured imprisonment, flogging, beating, stoning, hunger, thirst, and many other forms of suffering. If these were "light and momentary" afflictions, mine must be ultralight! Our complaints often seem petty in comparison with the hardships endured by great heroes of the faith.

THE OUTCOME OF OUR TRIALS

Testing times help us see *the value of our faith*. Faith, Peter says, is "of greater worth than gold" (1 Peter 1:7). Not only is gold beautiful; it is hard and durable—a symbol of permanence. Gold wedding rings last for centuries. But even gold, Peter says, "perishes even though refined by fire." Eventually all our money, jewelry, cars, clothes, and houses will disappear. But faith has enduring value.

Testing times help to prove *the authenticity of our faith*. Faith refined by fire "may be proved genuine" (v. 7). In its natural state, gold is often mixed with iron ore, granite, and other minerals. Every miner needs a refiner. A refiner's fire burns away inferior minerals that diminish the value of pure gold. Every believer needs a refiner too. God uses trials to refine and purify our faith so we can offer him more "praise, glory and honor" (v. 7; see also Job 23:10 and Proverbs 17:3.)

OUR ATTITUDE DURING TRIALS

How should believers view our problems? Without faith, we are tempted to see them as a trap or a barrier that prevents us from experiencing joy.

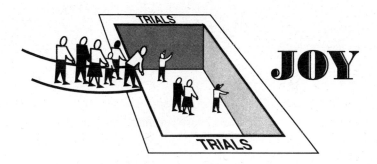

By faith, though, we can see our hardships in a more positive light. Instead of a box that locks us away from joy, trials are like a tunnel we pass through on our way to the greater joy of a more mature faith (Hebrews 12:2; Romans 5:3-5; James 1:2-4).

Peter writes, "Though you have not seen him, you love him; and even though you do not see him now, you believe in him and are filled with an inexpressible and glorious joy" (v. 8). Did you ever feel so joyful, so exuberant, that you could hardly contain yourself? Remarkably, Peter is writing to a suffering church, yet he seems to grope for words to describe the profound and "inexpressible joy" of serving Christ. "Glorious joy" translates the Greek *agalliasthe,* which means to exult or leap for joy. It's the same word used to describe the Philippian jailor's joy when he and his household believed in God (Acts 16:34), the joy of the saved in Heaven (Revelation 19:7), and even the joy that filled Jesus himself (Luke 10:21).

Is it really possible to love, believe, and rejoice in a Christ you've never even seen? Let me share a personal example. My wife Candy and I have three children. The first two were born to us; then we adopted our youngest daughter, Mindy. She came to us from Korea when she was four months old. Although we had not seen her, we already loved her, beginning with the moment our social worker told us she was coming. For months we eagerly anticipated her arrival. Then the long-awaited moment came when our family drove to Kennedy Airport in New York on a rainy December evening and waited the final hours for Mindy's Northwest Airlines jet to arrive. Her plane was delayed in Chicago—adding two more seemingly endless hours to our wait.

Finally, a smiling flight attendant carried the baby off the plane and placed her into my wife's arms. After a few minutes—and a lot of tears, laughs, and picture-taking—I got my chance to hold my new daughter as Candy handed her to me.

I'll never forget how Mindy looked that night—wrapped in a pink blanket, with a tuft of black hair sticking straight up from the back of her head. She had to be exhausted from her twenty-four-hour plane ride just ended. But as I carefully lifted her high above my head to greet my new daughter, Mindy broke into a big wide smile!

I loved my daughter long before I laid eyes on her, but now my love was more complete as I held her in my arms.

No, we haven't seen Jesus yet. But we love him, and we look forward to that wonderful day when our faith will turn to sight and we will see him just as he is (1 John 3:2). God's Old Testament prophets eagerly desired to know more about Christ's completed work on the cross. They served God as they spoke about "the sufferings of Christ and the glories that would follow," and in a sense they also served us. As Peter notes, "Even angels long to look into these things" (1 Peter 1:10-12; see also Matthew 13:16, 17 and Ephesians 3:4, 5).

TOO CLOSE FOR COMFORT

On July 6, 1986, the temperature hovered in the high nineties. Our family didn't own an air conditioner, so an aging exhaust fan in an upstairs bedroom offered our only relief from the heat. Thoughtlessly, my wife and I left the fan running as we rushed our children out the door and headed for church early that Sunday morning.

Later, we were eating lunch at a local restaurant when a friend from church hurried to our table and blurted out, "Dave, I hate to tell you this, but your house is on fire." We sped home to find our house surrounded by fire engines. Smoke billowed from a hole in the roof. My son's mattress had been tossed out a window in flames, and a pile of blackened clothing and melted plastic toys lay smoldering on the ground.

The firefighters blamed the fire on our overheated exhaust fan. Some folk blamed it on God: "Why did he let this happen to you?" But over the next few months, as we cleaned up the mess and rebuilt our house, we were amazed to find ourselves sustained and strengthened by God's presence and power. Friends called to offer encouragement and prayers; some provided meals; others offered new clothes and toys for our children. Our family emerged with a stronger faith in Christ, a keener ability to minister to others, and a greater sense of gratitude for our blessings.

Never underestimate what God can teach you when your faith is under fire.

NOTES: CHAPTER TWO

1. For a helpful explanation of the meaning of Christ's atoning death on the cross, see Jack Cottrell, *What the Bible Says About God the Redeemer* (Joplin: College Press, 1987), pp. 430-441.

2. Tacitus, *Annals*, 15:44.

CHAPTER THREE

What's the Difference?

1 Peter 1:13–2:10

How has Jesus Christ changed your life?

Even if you're not a Christian, Jesus has not left your life untouched. He sustains all nature by his power (Colossians 1:16, 17; Hebrews 1:3). His memorable words find their way into everyday speech ("our daily bread," "judge not," "do unto others as you would have them do unto you"). The calendars in the Western world date from the approximate time of his birth.

The love of Christ has motivated his followers to establish countless schools, orphanages, nursing homes, hospitals, and other benevolent works. (In the city where I live, we have hospitals called Good Samaritan, Bethesda, Deaconess, and Christ. But I've never heard of a hospital anywhere called Atheist General!)

The glory of Christ has inspired much of the world's great art, music, and literature. His Word has influenced laws and guided governments. It isn't an overstatement to say that Jesus Christ has changed history unlike any other before or after him. And if you're a Christian, Christ has changed every aspect of your life.

Christ changes our *priorities*. Your commitment to the Lord affects the way you spend your money and the way you use your time. The wealthy tax collector Zacchaeus, for example, was known as a "sinner" in Jericho, but he became a generous, unselfish benefactor after the Lord brought salvation to his house (Luke 19:1-10). A decision to follow Christ affects your choice of a career, and the way you do your job. It changes the way you look at other people, and causes you to be more willing to invest yourself in loving others.

Christ changes our *families*. Becoming a Christian deeply influences the way you treat your spouse, your parents, or your children. It changes the very criteria by which you select a mate in the first place.

Christ changes our *future*. What a difference it makes to know you're on your way to Heaven, not hell. What an important difference it makes to think about growing old and facing death when you are filled with a living hope rooted in Jesus' resurrection from the dead!

First Peter speaks plainly about Christ's ability to change lives. Just as all history can be divided into B.C. (Before Christ) and A.D. *(Anno Domini,* "in the year of our Lord"), our personal lives can be divided into two parts as well: what our lives were like "Before Christ" came into our hearts, and what our lives are like "After Deciding" to follow Jesus. Consider the contrasts displayed by the following chart, based on texts found in 1 Peter.

BEFORE CHRIST	AFTER DECIDING
You followed evil desires and lived in ignorance (1:14)	You strive for obedience and holiness (1:14, 15)
You had an empty way of life (1:18)	You've experienced the new birth and have a living hope (1:3)
You were not a chosen people (2:9)	You are the people of God (2:9)
You had not received mercy (2:10)	You have received mercy (2:10)
You were like sheep going astray (2:25)	You have returned to the shepherd and overseer of your souls (2:25)
You wasted time doing what pagans do (4:3)	You can spend your time doing more worthwhile and lasting things as you fulfill the will of God (4:2)

These great life-changes occur in us because of the great salvation we share in Christ. Peter talked about this in 1 Peter 1:1-12 as he described our salvation, which is so wonderful that even the Old Testament prophets and the angels of God long to understand it more (vv. 10-12). The word "therefore" in 1 Peter 1:13 links the second half of chapter one with Peter's introductory comments about our great salvation and our living hope.

OBEDIENCE REPLACES DISOBEDIENCE

Christ changes the way we think and act. This requires considerable adjustment.

A few years ago, the folk at the local highway department made some changes in the streets near my house. They took down a stop sign that had been there for years, and they installed a new stop sign in a place where there never had been one. For weeks, my neighbors and I struggled to adjust. We had to learn to stop where we used to rush ahead, and go where we used to stop!

Likewise, when you become a Christian there are sinful acts to stop doing, and godly behaviors to start doing. It can be a struggle to learn how to stop and go in response to God's leading. (Years after he accepted Christ, the apostle Paul still struggled with this—see Romans 7:14-25.) But we will be on the right track if we develop ready minds, obedient hearts, and a willingness to strive for holiness.

READY MINDS

"Prepare your minds for action," Peter says (1 Peter 1:13). Literally, it's "gird up the loins of your mind." Since people wore long flowing robes in biblical times, they had to pull up their garments and tuck them into belts around their waists so their legs could move freely (see Exodus 12:11; 1 Kings 18:46; Luke 12:35, KJV). For people living in those days, "Gird up the loins of your mind" was roughly equivalent to the way we say, "Roll up your sleeves and get to work."

Lazy minds will not rise to the tough challenges and hard choices Christians face in today's world. We need to know not only what to

think; we must know *how* to think. Mental self-discipline helps us ful-
fill what Jesus called the first and greatest commandment: to "love the
Lord your God" with all of your inner being, including your mind
(Matthew 22:37, 38).

OBEDIENT HEARTS

Just as a human parent delights in the willing obedience of a child
(compare Proverbs 23:15, 16, 24, 25), so does the heavenly Father
experience delight when our desire is to please him. Peter says to live
"as obedient children" (v. 14).

Our culture really isn't into obedience these days. There was a time
when people drove around with bumper stickers on their cars that
read, "Question Authority." Now the bumper stickers say, "*Ignore*
Authority." I can't imagine *Time* magazine putting their man or woman
of the year on the cover with a headline that said, "He Obeyed God."

Even in the church, obedience isn't exactly a hot topic. We rightly
don't want to become legalistic and authoritarian, and there's an
understandable desire to be "seeker sensitive." But we mustn't forget
that God is a seeker too—he seeks worshipers who will worship him
in spirit and truth (John 4:23, 24). He seeks followers who will recognize that there's a big difference between loving obedience and grudging legalism. He calls to us with the frank appeal, "If you love me,
keep my commandments." In fact, as John, the so-called apostle of
love, wrote, "This is love for God: to obey his commands. And his
commands are not burdensome" (1 John 5:3). The obedience God
seeks flows from a heart overflowing with gratitude for his grace, his
goodness, his holiness, and his Fatherly love.

When my son Matthew was about three years old, he rode with me
in my worn-out old 1970 Ford Maverick while I ran some errands. It
was a cold winter day, and my car battery had been acting up. We
returned to the car after stopping at the bank, and when I turned the
ignition key, the car was unresponsive. Actually, it responded—but it
wasn't what I wanted to hear. It made the faint clicking sound drivers
recognize as the sign of a dead battery.

Angrily, I exclaimed, "Oh, Matthew, the car is dead!"

And with that, my son burst into tears. I hadn't considered how scary it sounded for me to pronounce my car "dead" in the presence of a literal-minded three-year-old. (Looking back, I suppose he probably thought we'd have to dig a giant hole and bury my poor "dead car" right there in the bank parking lot!)

So I attempted to reassure my son. "It's OK, Matt," I said. I knew I had some jumper cables in the trunk, so I continued, "Look, Matt, I'm going to get out and jump the car, and then everything will be all right."

This time, my son's tears changed into laughter. He thought it would be great fun to watch Dad try to "jump the car"!

Eventually I was able to restart my car. In the meantime, I relearned an important lesson. Sometimes children don't understand what their fathers are up to! When we're young, our parents say and do many things we do not fully comprehend. Ultimately, though, loving parents usually have our own good in mind.

We may not always understand all the ways of our heavenly Father. But we must "trust and obey."

HOLY NONCONFORMITY

Obedience is anything but dull. God calls us to a wonderful, liberating kind of holy nonconformity. "Do not conform to the evil desires you had when you lived in ignorance," Peter writes (1 Peter 1:14). J. B. Philips translates this verse, "Don't let your character be moulded by the desires of your ignorant days." The word translated "conform" (*suschematizo,* "to form or mold after") is used only one other place in the New Testament—in Romans 12:2, which says, "Do not conform any longer to the pattern of this world, but be transformed by the renewing of your mind."

Christians have the opportunity to demonstrate to a watching world a refreshing freedom. We are not captives of tradition, always forced to uphold the prevailing customs of our society. Nor are we merely anti-establishment rebels, defining ourselves by reaction against the prevailing customs. We are neither slaves of our culture, nor slaves of the counterculture. We are free in Christ, concerned with the will of our

Master, free to align with our culture when it is right, and critique and challenge it when it is wrong.

In one sense, we are supposed to conform. The difference is, we no longer are to conform to the world. Now we must conform to the character of God. "But just as he who called you is holy, so be holy in all you do" (1 Peter 1:15). Strangely enough, when you begin to think and act more like the Lord does, the world will consider you a nonconformist!

It's common today to divide our lives into different compartments. But Peter says to be holy "in *all* you do" (1 Peter 1:15). Everything God does is holy. Likewise, God calls us to holiness in both "secular" and "spiritual" activities. We are to reflect God's holiness in our business dealings, our personal relationships—even the way we conduct ourselves at school, at work, and at sporting events.

Holy nonconformity is fitting for people who live as strangers here on earth "in reverent fear" (v. 17). God calls us to be reverent, not reckless.

"Reverence" may sound a bit dull and unappealing to modern ears, conjuring up images of somber, boring worship services led by unsmiling, dark-robed, out-of-touch church leaders (called "Reverend"). But sometimes I think today's church is better at mocking the old religious stereotypes than we are at really becoming true worshipers ourselves. It's easy to point out what's wrong with traditional worship; it's a bit more difficult to pour ourselves into discovering how to become more reverent people ourselves.

It's possible to be relevant and still be reverent. In fact, the more we know about the real God we serve, the more reverent and heartfelt will be our worship. In our increasingly irreverent age, it's time we Christians spend less energy battling over *styles* of worship (traditional versus contemporary) or *settings* for worship (formal versus informal buildings), and focus on the true *spirit* of worship (sincere, reverent praise for God). It's time to rediscover and preach about genuine personal holiness.

How would you feel if, as a hospital aide wheeled you in to the operating room for open-heart surgery, your surgeon walked past nonchalantly chewing bubble gum and complaining that he wanted to get this operation over with quickly so he could watch a football game on TV? How would you feel if the pilot of your airliner announced that he was ignoring all instructions from the control tower because he just felt like doing his own thing today? We don't appreciate a casual approach when lives are at stake. Why, then, are we so casual about God and his requirements?

True reverence is simply the natural result of taking God seriously. How can we do anything but stand in awe of our creator and judge who holds our eternity in his hands?

FREEDOM REPLACES FUTILITY

Peter goes on to describe another way Christ has changed our lives. We were "redeemed" (from the Greek *lutroo,* a term used for paying a debt, buying freedom for a slave, or purchasing release for someone held captive by an enemy). Christ paid our sin-debt and freed us from bondage to sin and death.

From what were we redeemed? Christ freed us, Peter says, from an "empty way of life" (v. 18). The Greek word translated "empty" (*mataios*) meant "futile, worthless, unfulfilling." Paul used the word in Titus 3:9 to describe foolish, pointless controversies, and he used it in 1 Corinthians 15:17 when he wrote, "if Christ has not been raised, your faith is *futile.*" In Greek versions of the Old Testament book of Ecclesiastes, the same word is used repeatedly to show how without God everything on earth is "vain" or "meaningless."

This empty way of life was "handed down to you from your forefathers" (v. 18). Traditions have some value, but religious beliefs aren't necessarily right simply because they have been handed down by your ancestors. No matter how much we cherish our family's ethnic or religious heritage, we must examine all our beliefs in light of Scripture and be careful not to be ensnared by empty human traditions (see Colossians 2:8).

With what were we redeemed? Not with "perishable things such as silver and gold . . . but with the precious blood of Christ" (vv. 18, 19).

Most people wouldn't think of silver and gold as good examples of perishable things. But even these metals fade in comparison with the sur-
passing value of Christ's blood.

The blood of Christ is precious because of *its cost to Jesus*. As the
spotless Lamb of God, he suffered unimaginable agony when he died
on the cross. His blood is precious because of *its effects on us*. Christ's
blood cleanses our consciences, gives us access to God in worship and
prayer, and purifies us from all sin (Hebrews 9:14; 10:19; 1 John 1:7).

His blood is precious also because of *its place in God's plan*. Just as
the Passover lamb was selected and set apart prior to its actual time of
sacrifice (Exodus 12:3-6), Christ was "chosen before the creation of
the world, but was revealed in these last times for your sake" (1 Peter
1:20).

The work of Christ is so significant that Peter writes, "Through him
[Christ] you believe in God" (v. 21).

Did you ever ponder the fact that the best single argument for the
existence of God is simply Jesus Christ himself? "Through him you
believe in God." Through his life, teachings, and miracles, Jesus
demonstrated the *fact* that God truly exists. And he showed what *kind*
of God exists—for God's justice, grace, love, and other attributes were
embodied in his Son (Colossians 2:9).

We believe in God for many reasons—the created world, the Bible,
our inner awareness of right and wrong, our longings for immortality—
but the best reason to believe in God is simply this: God made himself
known in human history, humbled himself by taking the form of a
man, and lived among us for a while (John 1:14-18; Philippians 2:5-
11). If you've ever struggled with doubt about God's existence, let
Christ free you from the futility of abstract philosophical arguments
that can take you only so far. Get to know Jesus. Through him you can
believe in God. As Jesus himself said, "Anyone who has seen me has
seen the Father" (John 14:9).

The December 1994 edition of *Life* magazine carried a cover picture
of Jesus, with the intriguing headline: "Who Was He?" Inside were
pages of quotes from various people who expounded their various
views on the identity of Christ. I had to chuckle, though, at the realiza-

tion that the magazine cover answered its own question. Who is Jesus? *Life!*

Are you tired of shallow, self-centered, surface-level relationships that suck the life out of you instead of filling you up? Christ frees his people to love others "deeply, from the heart" (1 Peter 1:22).

Are you tired of the emptiness and lack of fulfillment that comes from living in a world where death and despair seem to rule the day?

"All men are like grass,
       and all their glory is like the flowers of the field;
the grass withers and the flowers fall,
       but the word of the Lord stands forever"
(1 Peter 1:24, 25; see also Isaiah 40:6-8).

These observations are simple but profound. Spring's plush pasture fields eventually give way to the dormancy of winter. Beautiful bouquets

---

HOW DOES JESUS SET US FREE?

Evil desires no longer control us (1 Peter 1:14);
       we're free to bear good fruit (Galatians 5:22-24).

Empty traditions no longer rule over us (1 Peter 1:18);
       we're free to serve God from the heart (Mark 7:5-13;
       John 4:23, 24; Colossians 2:6-8).

Hopelessness no longer weakens us;
       now our "faith and hope are in God" (1 Peter 1:21).

Selfishness no longer confines us;
       now we can have "sincere love" for others (1 Peter 1:22).

Death no longer destroys us;
       now we enjoy new life through "the living and enduring
       word of God" (1 Peter 1:23-25; Hebrews 2:14, 15).

---

of roses eventually wither and lose their fragrance. Our own lives seem so fleeting as we slide unendingly toward the grave.

But Christ can change all that.

He frees us from the stranglehold of death so that we no longer face the unhappy prospect of fading away like summer grass or cut flowers. We need not fear the future because we've accepted the "imperishable seed" of his "living and enduring" Word (1 Peter 1:23-25).

A NEW HUNGER REPLACES OLD HABITS

Peter tells us to be "like newborn babies" (1 Peter 2:2). Why? It's natural to compare someone who has been born again (as described in 1 Peter 1:3 and 1:23) to a baby. Jesus used a little child to illustrate what God requires of those who enter his kingdom (Mark 10:13-16), and the apostle Paul said, "In regard to evil be infants, but in your thinking be adults" (1 Corinthians 14:20). The Lord wants to transform us so that we're filled with childlike innocence and purity instead of malice, deceit, hypocrisies (the Greek word is plural), envy, and slander (1 Peter 2:1).

In this context, however, Peter's main point is not a newborn baby's innocence, but a baby's hunger. Infants eagerly, relentlessly crave nourishment. Likewise, we must "crave pure spiritual milk." Peter's reference to milk (Greek *gala*, from which we get our word "galaxy," as in the Milky Way) is a ready symbol of health-giving nutrition in any culture. The word translated "spiritual" (Greek *logikos*) is related to our word for "logic" and could also mean "reasonable or sensible." The only other time it appears in the New Testament is in Romans 12:1, where the offering of our bodies to God is called a "reasonable service," or an act of "spiritual worship." The milk of God's Word is reasonable; it makes sense; it nourishes the inner being. It's the best imaginable "comfort food."

When our children were small, their hunger for milk was undeniable; it caused my wife and me to lose lots of sleep by providing countless late-night bottles. Now that our kids are teenagers, they eat even more (as our grocery bills will attest)! Likewise, Christians need to find ways to maintain and grow in our hunger for spiritual nutrition. If your hunger is waning, talk to someone about it, take a personal retreat, spend a day in fasting and prayer, ask God to "restore to me the joy of your salvation" (Psalm 51:12).

Those who have "tasted that the Lord is good" have good reason never to be indifferent about God's Word (1 Peter 2:3; see also Psalm 34:8). The word for *good* (Greek *chrestos*) is only one letter different from the word for Christ, *Christos*. The early Christians sometimes encouraged one another with a little play on words. They would say, "Christos chrestos"—"Christ is good." Jesus used the word *chrestos* when he said his yoke is "easy" (Matthew 11:30). Any demand the Lord places upon us is kind. It's good. It is "easy" in the sense that it fits us well.

It's only natural for a Christian to crave a deeper relationship with this One who changed our lives for the better.

GREAT HONORS REPLACE
GREAT HOPELESSNESS

Jason Li grew up in Communist China. Brought up as an atheist, he assumed that only the weak and naive believed in God. But his life changed in 1993 when he came to the United States to study chemistry at the University of Cincinnati. Scott and Ann Ellis, volunteers with University Christian Church's outreach ministry to international students, met Jason at the airport and invited him to spend the night in their home. Over the next several days, Jason ate his meals at the Ellis's family table. They helped him find an apartment to rent, showed him around the city, and explained American customs. They introduced him to neighbors and other university students. And they invited him to church.

In short, they truly became his friends.

Jason had never owned or read a Bible before, nor had he heard Christians pray or sing. The friendliness and love of God's people impressed him—and frightened him a bit, as well.

One day I preached on John 3:16. Jason rushed up to me after the service and exclaimed, "I have never heard what you told us today about the importance of believing in Jesus."

I asked, "Would you like to talk more about this?"

He said, "Yes."

We met twice on Tuesday evenings in the church office, as I carefully discussed with him what it means to be a Christian. Near the end of our second session, Jason told me he wanted to be baptized. Though I was rejoicing inside, I wanted to make sure he understood the importance of a personal commitment to Christ, especially since everything was so new to him.

I began to review the basics of the gospel. Finally Jason stopped me in mid-sentence. His eyes flashed intently as he told me with conviction, "I know it's not easy to be a Christian. I know it will be especially hard when I return to China someday. But I will be loyal to Jesus for the rest of my life!"

Tears stung my eyes as I listened to Jason's sincere good confession. Soon afterward, our church family rejoiced together around a swimming pool as Jason Li, our new brother in Christ, emerged from the waters of baptism.[1]

In some ways, Jason's story is unique. But in a way, it's my story too—and yours.

All of us who come to Christ move from purposelessness to privilege, from hopelessness to honor.

Once we were outside of God's saving mercy. Even when we didn't realize it, we were wallowing in darkness and despair. But in Christ, things have changed. We've become new creations. Now we are "living stones" God uses to build a holy house where he will dwell (1 Peter 2:4, 5; see also 1 Corinthians 3:16, 17). We're no longer adrift, unanchored, unstable. Jesus is the living stone on which we build our lives. (Notice the daring metaphor—stones usually aren't alive, but Christ has both the solid, sturdy qualities of a rock and the dynamic, growing qualities of life.)[2] Jesus is the foundation and the cornerstone of our faith (vv. 6-8; see also Matthew 16:18; Acts 4:10-12). He is our great high priest, and we are "a holy priesthood, offering spiritual sacrifices acceptable to God through Jesus Christ" (v. 5).

Jesus is the greatest somebody who ever walked the earth. So if we are his disciples, we certainly aren't nobodies! Christ has transformed us. Now we are "a chosen people, a royal priesthood, a holy nation, a people belonging to God," here to fulfill a special purpose: to declare God's praises in a dark world (vv. 9, 10).

Jesus is in the business of changing lives. What difference has he made in you? What's the difference you will make in the world?

NOTES: CHAPTER THREE

1. I related this story about Jason Li in a previously published article, "They're Coming to America," in *The Restoration Herald* (July, 1995).

2. Wayne Grudem, *1 Peter* (Grand Rapids: Eerdmans, 1988), p. 98.

CHAPTER FOUR

Small Steps and
Giant Leaps

1 Peter 2:11-25

D o you like parades? When I was growing up on a farm in
southern Ohio, my brothers and I always looked forward to a
special day once a year when our parents took us to see a big
parade.

It wasn't the Rose Bowl Parade in Pasadena, or the Macy's
Thanksgiving Day Parade in New York City. No, it was the annual
Labor Day parade in the small town of Lynchburg, Ohio. But to me,
that parade was exciting stuff!

There were marching bands from the local schools, complete with
squeaky clarinets, at least one badly out-of-step trombonist, and
majorettes who sometimes dropped their batons (but no one minded).
Youth groups from local churches paraded down the street on flatbed
trucks converted to floats for the occasion, complete with colored tis-
sue paper poked through chicken wire frames. People on horseback
threw bubble gum and pennies to children in the crowd. And at the
end of the parade came freshly shined red fire trucks from the
Lynchburg Volunteer Fire Department, with their sirens screeching.

Everyone likes a parade. Even the ancient Romans liked parades.
When one of their generals came home after a successful campaign,
the people lined the streets of Rome and joined in celebrations called
"Triumphs" or "Triumphal Processions." The crowds cheered, scattered
flowers along the road, and burned spices and incense that billowed
through the air like a sweet-smelling cloud.

The apostle Paul used the joy and excitement of a parade to picture the kind of victory celebration we share as Christians: "But thanks be to God, who always leads us in triumphal procession in Christ and through us spreads everywhere the fragrance of the knowledge of him" (2 Corinthians 2:14).

I'm often fascinated by the kind of expansive language used in the Bible. Paul's words are a good example. Does he really mean that God "*always* leads us in triumphal procession"? Can we live triumphant, victorious lives as followers of Christ all the time? Even when we're at work or school? Even when our government leaders seem to be failing us, and our culture seems to be drifting farther and farther from God?

The answer is a resounding "Yes!" We can march in the Lord's victory parade even during the daily grind. In 1 Peter 2:11-25, Peter shows how we can at least take some small steps of victory, even in the midst of hardships. By following in the footsteps of Jesus, we can take some giant leaps forward in our walk of faith.

A CITIZEN'S STEPS

I'll never forget the day my daughter Mindy became a United States citizen. Since she was from Korea, we had to fill out a lot of paperwork for the Immigration and Naturalization Service and formally apply for her to become a naturalized citizen. The final step was to take her to a special court session in Brooklyn, New York, where she and I sat in a large room filled with people of all ages from all over the world—all of whom were becoming citizens or helping friends celebrate their new citizenship.

We listened as a black-robed judge enthusiastically talked to everyone about the privileges and responsibilities of citizenship. Then, in a touching moment, the entire crowd stood, and all of us—including my two-year-old daughter—raised our right hands and promised loyalty to our country, then repeated the Pledge of Allegiance to the United States flag. I have always been glad to be a citizen of this great nation, but that day stirred a new kind of gladness as I heard my little girl proudly exclaim, "I'm an Am-aw-i-can!"

In a sense, Christians have a twofold citizenship. We have privileges and responsibilities in two different realms. We are citizens on earth, but our higher citizenship is in the kingdom of God, which transcends any geographical or ethnic boundaries. Jesus resisted the ambitious efforts of some political enthusiasts who tried to make him king (John 6:15). But he made it clear, nonetheless, that he did come to rule—over a kingdom which is "not of this world" (John 18:36, 37).

The apostle Paul enjoyed the benefits of being a citizen of the Roman empire (Acts 16:37; 21:39). He was born a citizen, while others (like a Roman army officer mentioned in Acts 22:28), paid a big price for citizenship. But Paul saw that the privileges of Roman citizenship faded in comparison with his higher and more important citizenship. He said, "Our citizenship is in Heaven. And we eagerly await a Savior from there, the Lord Jesus Christ" (Philippians 3:20).

CITIZENS OF HEAVEN

Since we are children of God, we are *aliens in a strange place* (1 Peter 2:11)—temporary residents, visitors who look forward to our permanent home.

In September, 1996, astronaut Shannon Lucid returned to earth after a record-setting stay of 188 days in space on the Mir space station. Her long-awaited return home was delayed even more than expected because of equipment trouble and hurricanes. But she remained remarkably upbeat and nonchalant about her endurance feat, saying simply, "I've had a great time here [on the space station]. But obviously I'm very, very anxious to go back to my real home back in Houston, Texas, with my family."[1]

Though most of us haven't traveled in space, I think a lot of us understand a bit of how Shannon Lucid felt. Even when we're having a good time here on earth, there's something in us that longs to go to our real home—our eternal, heavenly abiding place with God.

In a sense, we are always aliens. Here on earth, we will always experience some kind of alienation. Before we came to Christ, our sins alienated us from God. We were "separate from Christ, excluded from citizenship in Israel and foreigners to the covenants of the promise, without hope and without God in the world" (Ephesians 2:12). After accepting the Lord, we are no longer alienated from God; we are "fellow citizens with God's people and members of God's household" (Ephesians 2:19). But then things take another interesting twist: once we stop being aliens in relation to God, we become alienated from the world as we take our stand for Christ.

I remember hearing the story about a veteran missionary who retired after years of hard, sacrificial service. Returning home from the foreign mission field, he happened to be on the same ocean liner as the President of the United States. The missionary disembarked from the ship as an excited crowd cheered for the President, with military colors flying and greetings from important dignitaries. Tearfully, the missionary leaned toward his wife and said, "I have given my life to serve the Lord in a difficult place, and no one came here to welcome me home and shower me with love and rewards." His wife replied, "But, dear, you're not home yet."

Until we get to Heaven, we're not home yet.

In the meantime, we are *soldiers in a hostile place*, battling against "sinful desires, which war against your soul" (1 Peter 2:11). We live in an environment that is hostile toward godliness. Among Christians today, there's a lot of talk about spiritual warfare involving angels and demons. But it may be that the most common, and the most troublesome form of spiritual warfare is the everyday battleground of temptation we face on a personal level as our souls are besieged by sinful desires (see James 4:1).

The Greek word (*strateuo*) that we translate "wage war" is a military term. In ancient armies, there were leaders called *strategei* who planned military maneuvers to defeat the enemy. (This is the origin of our English word "strategy.") The same word appears in 2 Timothy 2:4 to describe how Christians are like soldiers engaged in active service for Christ, our commanding officer. Apparently, our sinful desires are in active service too—Satan's strategic tools to overwhelm and defeat us. We repel these desires by submitting ourselves to the Lord and by resisting the devil (James 4:7).

As citizens of Heaven, we also are *ambassadors in a strategic place*. Do your Christian convictions ever make you feel like an alien in your workplace, at school, or in your neighborhood? Do you feel like you don't fit in? Don't despair. It may be that you're exactly where God wants you to be. You have a job to do right where you are: "Live such good lives among the pagans that, though they accuse you of doing wrong, they may see your good deeds and glorify God on the day he visits us" (1 Peter 2:12).

Notice where Peter insists we are to live good lives: "among the pagans." We aren't called to live in isolation. We are "in the world, but not of the world" (John 17:14-18), called to live pure and blameless lives and hold forth the Word of life in a dark and crooked world (Philippians 2:14, 15).

This idea has a number of practical implications for people who are serious about following in Jesus' steps. For example, instead of fleeing from the inner cities, we need to see them as potential outposts for Christian influence. Instead of simply bemoaning the secularism and wickedness of today's university campuses, we must establish strategic ministries on these very campuses which can shine the light of Christ to searching students.

In our moments of weariness, it might sound appealing for Christians to shun all contact with unbelievers, but it is God's strategy for us to live among them and infiltrate Satan's enemy camp with the gospel so that our detractors will eventually become Christians themselves.

Churches dare not engage in a sad game of "hide and seek" in which our members hide behind the walls of the church building, timidly inviting outsiders to seek the treasure hidden inside. That's the very opposite of Christ's command to go into all the world and preach the gospel.

We can't seek the lost from the safe confines of our Christian subculture. But if we're willing to look, we'll find plenty of people in need—in prisons and in mansions, in crowded apartment buildings and isolated cabins, on city streets and country roads, in high schools, and in nursing homes.

I rejoice because of Christians I know who are faithfully "living good lives among the pagans;" people like Howard and Kathy Taylor, who in their retirement years moved to Brooklyn to help plant a church and administer a Christian preschool program; people like Matt Cooper, who has developed a unique outreach ministry called "Meaningless Enterprises" to help young people who have doubts about Christianity; people like James Lane, who has served for years in a dual role as preacher for an inner city church and as director of an urban housing development program in Hartford, Connecticut.

We cannot salt the earth if we remain inside the saltshaker. We will not light the world if we hide our lights under a basket. All of us need to engage our culture and reach our neighbors. That's part of what it means to follow in Jesus' steps.

CITIZENS OF EARTH

Though Christians are citizens of Heaven, we are citizens of earth too, with several responsibilities to fulfill toward our fellow citizens and our government authorities. Peter sums up our duties in two words that are simple to say but hard to do: "Submit yourselves" (v. 13).

Why submit? "For the Lord's sake" (v. 13). A Christian needs no other reason than this. It honors the Lord when we humbly respect authority; it dishonors him when we are rebellious and disobedient.

To whom should we submit? "To every authority instituted among men" (v. 13). Specifically, Peter mentions kings and governors. But in light of other Scriptures, the principle probably applies more broadly as well (Romans 13:1-7; Titus 3:1). Christians are to practice healthy sub-mission in various realms of personal relationships: at home, at school, at work, and in the church.

Of course, this raises some challenging questions for believers living under the rule of less-than-ideal governments. Must Christians submit even to evil emperors like Nero? To paranoid demagogues like Herod? To sly political opportunists like Pilate? A few years ago, I taught a group of church leaders in Haiti. It was interesting to listen to the insights of these Haitian brethren who struggled to be both faithful Christians and submissive citizens. They were living under an oppres-sive and confusing government that had systematically stripped away the people's freedom and wealth for years. The principles of 1 Peter

2:13 were difficult, but not impossible, for these Christians to apply.

Of course, you don't have to go to Haiti to find an oppressive and confusing government! Even in a place of comparative freedom like the United States, it's frustrating for Christians when our highest court refuses to grant legal protection to the lives of unborn babies, and when some of our elected officials seem more interested in their personal popularity in the polls than in doing what is right. It's sad when our leaders opt for expediency over integrity, money instead of morality, fame rather than faith, and power instead of principle.

In our imperfect land, Christians can do more than merely gripe about our government. We can pray (1 Timothy 2:1); we can protest (Acts 16:35-40; 25:7-12); and we can participate by voting or by running for office.

According to 1 Peter 2:14, God planned for government to fulfill two primary functions: punishment of those who do wrong, and commendation of those who do right. In other words, governing officials must be concerned about justice—for both offending criminals and law-abiding citizens. Ideally, our legal system should function with complete fairness and reasonable swiftness. "When the sentence for a crime is not quickly carried out, the hearts of the people are filled with schemes to do wrong" (Ecclesiastes 8:11). Government's role is to protect the rights of the innocent and establish an environment where peaceful, godly lives can flourish (1 Timothy 2:2).

Obviously, there are limits to how much a Christian should submit. When the pharaoh of Egypt told the Hebrew midwives to kill all newborn Hebrew boys, they refused, acknowledging the divinely appointed value of human life (Exodus 1:17). God's great servant Moses was preserved by his mother's brave act of civil disobedience (Exodus 2:1-10). Daniel and his friends, Shadrach, Meshach, and Abednego disregarded government orders when the king commanded them to worship idols (thus they refused to engage in a sin of commission) or stop praying to God (thus they refused to engage in a sin of omission). God protected and blessed these faithful men for what they did (Daniel 3, 6).

Perhaps the most interesting example of civil disobedience is one in which Peter himself was involved. When the Jewish leaders ordered the

apostles to stop preaching and teaching in Jesus' name, Peter refused
to comply with their orders and continued to obey the Lord's Great
Commission. Yes, this was the same apostle who wrote, "Submit yourselves for the Lord's sake to every authority." But when the authorities
directly contradicted a clear command of Christ, Peter's response was
clear: "We cannot help speaking about what we have seen and heard"
(Acts 4:20), and "We must obey God rather than men" (Acts 5:29).
Jesus' command, "Go and teach," supersedes anyone else's order to
"Stop teaching."

For people following in the footsteps of Jesus, loyal, respectful citizenship is the norm. We must abide by our nation's laws. Civil disobedience must be the rare exception—prayerfully, conscientiously applied
in unusual circumstances with great care that our genuine motivation
is for God to be glorified in our actions.

When Christians conduct ourselves responsibly as citizens of our
nation, there are three positive results.

• *We silence ignorant talk.* "For it is God's will that by doing good you
should silence the ignorant talk of foolish men" (1 Peter 2:15). The
word for "silence" (Greek *phimoo*) could also be translated "muzzle."
(The same word is used in 1 Corinthians 9:9 for muzzling an ox, and
in Matthew 22:34 for the way Jesus "silenced" his opponents the
Sadducees.) Ignorance often is quite vocal, but accusations of wrongdoing sound hollow when a person is known as a steady example of
faithfulness. When Christians are good citizens, we give our critics one
less thing to complain about. The best way to silence our critics is simply to do good.

• *We demonstrate the proper use of freedom.* "Live as free men, but do
not use your freedom as a cover-up for evil; live as servants of God" (1
Peter 2:16). It's interesting that Peter says to submit to authority, then
immediately afterward he says to live as free men. Submission is not
the opposite of freedom, as some suppose. Rightly understood, submission actually paves the way to greater liberty. In Christ we are free
from slavery to sin, free from the oppressive power of guilt, free from
sin's permanent death sentence, free to serve God wholeheartedly. But
we are not totally free to make our own rules! God grants us the free-

dom to decide whether we will *do* right or wrong, but not the responsibility to determine what *is* right and wrong.

Do you enjoy riding on a roller coaster? A roller-coaster ride can produce an exhilarating feeling of freedom as you whirl around hairpin turns with your hands extended, the wind blowing in your hair, surrounded by people who are yelling at the top of their lungs. But a roller coaster is fun only as long as it stays on the track. In fact, if a roller coaster left the track, it would result in serious injury or even death. You're free to enjoy the ride only as long as you stay on the right track. Similarly, God calls us to enjoy the exhilarating spiritual freedom that comes when we stay on the right track and obey the truth of Christ (John 8:32, 36).

• *We establish a healthy climate for relationships with others.* "Show proper respect to everyone: Love the brotherhood of believers, fear God, honor the king" (1 Peter 2:17).

Small steps like these—respect, love, reverence, honor—could lead to giant leaps forward in our culture if every citizen took them seriously.

A WORKER'S STEPS

Just as we are to follow in Jesus' footsteps in our relationship with civil authorities, we must obey our Lord in the workplace. In 1 Peter 2:18-20, Peter gives instructions to slaves about their relationships with their masters.⁴ It's important to keep in mind that he is writing to people who had no rights of self-determination about their own careers. As slaves, these folk couldn't resign their jobs, search the want ads, and find other employers. What could Peter say to encourage people who possessed no legal or economic freedom—who in some cases were stuck in difficult and oppressive working conditions? If his words are hard for our modern ears to hear, remember that he was writing to help believers live victoriously for Christ under a repressive (and at least at that time in history, unchangeable) labor system.

"Submit yourselves to your masters with all respect, not only to those who are good and considerate, but also to those who are harsh" (v. 18). It's much easier, of course, to submit to a kind and considerate boss. But, realistically, some bosses who have authority over our work may be harsh at times or even "crooked." The word translated "harsh" (Greek *skolios*) is the basis of our word "scoliosis," which describes a curvature of the spine. It's very difficult if you find yourself working every day for an employer who is crooked, difficult, mean-spirited, and dishonest. Christian employees must not obey the boss if doing so requires them to sin. But the overall attitude of a Christian worker must begin with respectful cooperation.

Ben, a company vice president, was dismayed when he saw a contract in his desk's "in box" waiting for his signature. Since the contract represented the final stage of a lucrative business deal for Ben's company, signing it was a "no-brainer" in financial terms. But the terms of the contract were subtly dishonest, and as a Christian, Ben couldn't sign those papers in good conscience. Yet he would incur his boss's wrath, and possibly lose his job, if he refused to sign.

It's easy to say what you *should* do in a situation like this, but it's not easy if your own career is on the line. Ben courageously confronted his boss, refused to sign the papers, and waited for the outcome. After a day or two, Ben's boss revised the contract, eliminated the deceptive wording, and commended Ben for his honesty.

Not every such situation turns out so well. Throughout history, Christians like Ben sometimes have lost their jobs when they took a stand for principles over pragmatism. In the first century, many believers had to endure the pain of unjust suffering because they were "conscious of God" (vv. 19, 20). When we have the opportunity to confront a corrupt employer with his wrongdoing, certainly it's right to do so. Sometimes we may need to find a different job. But when suffering on the job is unavoidable, there's great comfort in knowing that our earthly masters are accountable to the Master in Heaven who ultimately will make sure that justice is done (Colossians 3:22–4:1).

THE SAVIOR'S STEPS

It's in this context (a believer's responsibility to persevere even during times of undeserved suffering) that Peter wrote the memorable

words, "To this you were called, because Christ suffered for you, leav-
ing you an example, that you should follow in his steps" (1 Peter
2:21). If you ever face hardship under an oppressive government or an
unfair employer, it helps to remember that Christ suffered too. Jesus is
not like a military general who stays far away in a safe fortress while his
troops fight and bleed on the battlefield; he is right there with us in
the midst of the battle.

In his commentary on 1 Peter, Alan Stibbs pointed out that the Lord
taught three basic facts about suffering. First, suffering was a necessary
part of his work as Messiah (Luke 24:25-27, 44-47). Second, his suffering was for others, as a ransom to provide forgiveness of sins
(Matthew 20:28; 26:28). Third, his followers must similarly be prepared to suffer (Mark 8:34; 10:38, 39).

Peter brings out these same three points when he writes, "Christ
suffered . . . for you, . . . that you should follow in his steps" (1 Peter
2:21).[3]

The word translated "example" (Greek *hupogrammos*) means "something written underneath." Perhaps we could picture in our minds a
child's coloring book that contains bold, dark lines to trace. Christ's
footsteps boldly mark the path we must walk. He set a flawless example of sinlessness. Even when he was crucified, Jesus did not resort to
deceit or threats of retaliation; instead, he continued to entrust himself
to the Father (1 Peter 2:22, 23; compare Isaiah 53:6-12; Matthew
27:12-44).

In the process, he "bore our sins in his body on the tree" (1 Peter
2:24). The reference to Christ's body underscores the fact that his
physical death was necessary for sins to be forgiven, just as animals
shed their blood under the old covenant. It also highlights the fact that
Jesus' sacrifice was real—a matter of flesh and blood—a genuine historical event, not a religious myth. His wounds bring us healing, and
through him we are restored to "the Shepherd and Overseer" of our
souls (v. 25).

It's interesting that *Peter* wrote this wonderful passage about the
meaning of the Lord's suffering. There once was a time when Peter was
so uncomfortable with the idea of Jesus' death, he rebuked the Lord

for even talking about it (Matthew 16:21-23). But by the time he wrote this epistle, it's clear that Peter had gotten the message! Peter had taken some giant leaps in his own growth as he walked in the footsteps of Jesus.

Luke 7 tells about a time when Jesus visited a town called Nain. As the Lord and his disciples drew near to Nain, they were met by a funeral procession coming out of the town the other direction. It's a sad scene. A man (presumably, a young man) had died. Near the front of the funeral procession marched the dead man's mother. She had experienced the sorrow of death before, for Luke notes that she was a widow. And the Bible adds poignantly that this fellow who had died was her *only* son. It's not hard to imagine the heartache that filled her soul.

Can you picture the scene as these two processions of people met outside the village gate of Nain? As Jesus and his disciples approached the town, the faces in their crowd probably looked eager, interested, excited about what Jesus was doing and saying. But look at the sad, mournful faces of those in the other procession—the people coming out of the town to bury the dead man. What will happen when these two parades of people meet on the road—one a procession of death with a corpse at the front, the other a procession of joy led by the Lord of life?

Luke records that when Jesus saw the widow, his heart went out to her. He told her, "Don't cry." Then in a dramatic demonstration of his power, he reached out and touched the dead man's coffin (the pallet or stretcher on which the body was carried). More than mere physical contact, the Greek word translated "touched" suggests a strong, powerful intervention. Jesus grasped the coffin with a firm grip of authority, as if to grab Satan by the collar and say, "You're not going to win this battle!" Then Jesus spoke to the man, "Young man, I say to you, get up!" And immediately, "the dead man sat up and began to talk, and Jesus gave him back to his mother" (Luke 7:11-15).

There were no longer two processions outside of Nain that day— one that was happy and one that was sad. No, now there was just one big celebration of life and resurrection. The march of death ran head-on into the Lord of life, and Jesus turned that funeral procession into a triumphal procession.

Aren't you glad he still does?

If Jesus can handle the enormous challenge of overcoming death, surely he can also handle the challenges you face today. Don't be disheartened if your faith is under fire. Take some steps in the footsteps of Jesus. Even little steps count. Be an involved and helpful citizen. Show respect for your boss and fellow employees.

The Lord is leading a victory parade. You can march in it if you're willing. Just follow in his steps.

NOTES: CHAPTER FOUR

1. Marcia Dunn, "Lucid Says, 'So Long, Space,'" *The Cincinnati Enquirer*, September 24, 1996, p. A8.

2. Here Peter does not use the words *doulos*, "slave" or *diakonos*, "servant." Instead, he employs the word *oiketes*, which carries the idea of household service (from *oikos*, "house"). Though household servants like these did not enjoy the freedoms we possess today, many of them were reasonably well-trained and some were treated like members of the master's family. The word translated "masters" (*despotai*) is the word from which we derive our word *despot*, and suggests a very strong form of sovereign authority. See Wayne Grudem, *1 Peter* (Grand Rapids: Eerdmans, 1900), pp. 123, 124.

3. Alan Stibbs, *The First Epistle of Peter* (Grand Rapids: Eerdmans, 1976), p. 116.

CHAPTER FIVE

Welcome, Jesus, to Our Home

1 Peter 3:1-12

I first learned about my wife's suitcase when we packed the car for our honeymoon. You've heard of American Tourister luggage? This bag was an American disaster. It was olive green (quite the popular color when we got married in 1975), with latches that barely closed (due to the way Candy had repeatedly crammed it too full over the years).

Me? I traveled lightly—stuffing my T-shirts, sneakers, sweat socks, and razor into a duffel bag. By contrast, my wife's suitcase was enormous. She filled it with what seemed to me an amazing array of extra things: panty hose, a curling iron, an industrial-strength blow dryer, and a bottle of foul-smelling nail polish remover. I teased Candy mercilessly about her heavy suitcase whenever I lugged it to the car and crammed it into the trunk.

I said, "Wow, when I married you I didn't realize all this stuff came along with you!"

But later, after we were married a while, it dawned on me that I had brought my own "suitcase" into our marriage as well. My baggage wasn't literally a suitcase. It was just a big pile of likes and dislikes, good and bad habits, and realistic and unrealistic expectations I had developed over the years. In fact, I've concluded that everyone who marries brings along a trunkload of "betrothal baggage" into the relationship. Our baggage includes ideas and behaviors we picked up from our parents, our previous dating experiences, the standard of living we're accustomed to enjoying, our spiritual maturity levels, our ethnic and cultural backgrounds, and our friendships with others. On the good side, the baggage includes our God-given personality traits and spiritual gifts. On the not-so-good side, the baggage usually includes some "sin that so easily entangles" (Hebrews 12:1), plenty of personal immaturity, and often some skeletons in the family closet.

If you come into a partnership already "bent out of shape," it's no wonder marriage is filled with more adjustments than a chiropractor's office. But it's possible to make marriage work, even in today's high-pressure world when families are under fire.

In the midst of all the bad news about high divorce rates, troubled children, and other indications of dysfunction, there's hope for our families if we welcome Jesus to our homes. And there are encouraging signs that couples are hungry to renew the kind of family commitments that will make our communities, churches, and nations strong. For example, according to an article in *U.S. News & World Report* (July 1, 1996) called "The Myth of AWOL Parents," parents today actually spend about the same amount of time with their children as parents did in 1965. And an article entitled "Monogamy Underestimated?" cites the results of a Gallup poll published in 1990 showing that marital infidelity is less common than is often supposed. Fewer than one married person in ten has been unfaithful to his or her spouse; four out of five say they would marry the same person again; and 60 percent of married couples say they pray together.[1]

While marriage and parenting are seldom easy, we'd certainly be better off if we more consciously and more consistently invited Jesus to be Lord of our homes! The Lord gave us some helpful instructions about marriage in 1 Peter 3, and this text comes alive when we recall that, in addition to being inspired by God, Peter knew from experience what it was like to be a married man.

Evidently Peter took his wife along on some of his missionary travels (1 Corinthians 9:5). We don't know a lot about the marriage of Peter and his wife, but we can assume that it wasn't easy to be married to an apostle—especially one with the temperament of Simon Peter! We do know that when Peter welcomed Jesus into his home, the Lord cured Peter's mother-in-law of a fever (Mark 1:29-31).

Jesus brought healing grace to Peter's house, and if we'll heed the instructions of 1 Peter 3, God's grace will bless our homes as well.

WISE WORDS FOR WIVES

This section of Scripture begins with the phrase, "in the same way" or "likewise" (Greek *homoios*). "In the same way" as *what?* Peter is pointing back to the example of Jesus described in the previous section of his letter (1 Peter 2:21-25). Just as Jesus submitted to the Father's will, and just as Christians are to demonstrate a proper attitude both in relation to civil government and in the workplace, the family is another realm of human relationship where respectful, cooperative behavior is needed.

A HEALTHY KIND OF SUBMISSION

"Wives, . . . be submissive," Peter writes (3:1). This certainly doesn't mean the wife becomes the husband's slave. New Testament scholar I. Howard Marshall explains: *"In the same way* simply takes up the theme of submission that was already discussed in 2:13 and 18. This phrase does not put wives on the same level as slaves, but requires them to show submission in the way appropriate to their situation."[2] In the poetic words of Robert Burns:

Husband, husband, cease your strife.
  No longer idly rave, Sir.
Though I am your wedded wife,
  I am not your slave, Sir.

Both men and women are commanded, "Submit yourselves for the Lord's sake" (1 Peter 2:13). Scripture doesn't shrink back, however, from focusing special attention on the submission of the wife (Ephesians 5:22-24; Colossians 3:18). Sadly, men have sometimes misused Scriptures like these to justify chauvinism and mistreatment of women. Others have reacted so strongly in the opposite direction that for all practical purposes they deny that verses like these are in the Bible at all. As we should do with any portion of God's Word, we must be careful to interpret and apply the text responsibly and in harmony with other verses on the subject, not merely find ways to substantiate our own biases. The challenge is to discover a healthy way to live out God's good intentions in all our relationships, not simply to throw out the baby with the bath water because we feel uncomfortable with a word like "submission."

Rightly understood, submission is not degrading. It doesn't diminish one's dignity or personhood. The root meaning of the Greek *hupotasso* ("to submit" or "subject oneself") was "to arrange oneself under." The submissive person lives in a proper arrangement with others. Rightly understood, submission suggests an attitude of humility, thoughtfulness, and consideration. A submissive person puts love into action by unselfishly doing whatever is in the best interests of another person. Submission means conducting oneself with cooperation and respect, "yielding the right of way" to others instead of demanding to have your own way.

Submission certainly didn't diminish the greatness of Jesus Christ. He submitted to God the Father, yet was equal to him. In fact, Christ's submission was actually a key to his greatness (Philippians 2:5-11).

Notice, Peter doesn't say, "Wives, be inferior to your husbands," or "Wives, act like doormats so your husbands can walk all over you." Later in this same chapter, Peter makes it clear that the Christian wife is just as much a child of God as her husband is (3:7). A wise Christian husband will never abuse his wife, but will do everything he can to assist her in fulfilling God's will. Scripture couldn't be clearer: "Husbands, love your wives and do not be harsh with them" (Colossians 3:19). Whatever else God meant by instructing women to be submissive, he certainly didn't intend that submission should be a weapon men use to justify harsh or abusive behavior.

Ultimately, the head of the house is not the husband, but Christ himself. (As someone has said, the issue isn't who rules the roost, but who rules the rooster.)

Yes, Christian husbands must take the lead in our homes. But we also are obligated to love our wives sacrificially, "as Christ loved the church and gave himself up for her" (Ephesians 5:25). When men endeavor to lay down their lives this way, it makes their wives' submission easier, even joyful—the natural response of a person who feels secure in another's love. In a healthy Christian marriage, the husband and wife are engaged in a circle of self-giving, not a selfish tug-of-war.

AN EFFECTIVE KIND OF EVANGELISM

But what about the many couples who aren't enjoying "a healthy Christian marriage"? And what about women who are married to non-Christian men? How can they cope? What do the Scriptural admonitions about submission mean in their case?

Scripture warns against becoming "unequally yoked" with unbelievers (2 Corinthians 6:14-16). But, as is still sometimes the case today, there were women in the first-century church who had accepted Christ

---

HOW CAN THE CHURCH HELP "UNEQUALLY YOKED" SPOUSES?

1. Provide lots of encouragement. A person married to a non-Christian often feels discouraged. There may be tension in the house when the Christian leaves home for worship. Perhaps he would like to attend a weekend retreat, a Christian convention, or a weekly Bible study, but his spouse doesn't understand or approve. Or a Christian wife may feel frustrated because her husband refuses to share in times of family worship, discuss spiritual matters, or even to pray at the dinner table. It helps if other Christian friends are sensitive to these special hurts and offer genuine encouragement.

2. Help nurture their children in the Lord. If kids lack the attention of a godly father, for example, they will need some extra attention from men in the church who can provide role models of masculine faith.

3. Reach out to their spouses. Provide opportunities for non-Christian family members to get acquainted with people from the

---

after they were married, while their husbands remained in unbelief. Scripture plainly states that a person married to an unbelieving spouse should not seek to end the marriage, as long as the unbelieving partner is willing to stay (1 Corinthians 7:12, 13). But how can a woman submit herself to a selfish, unbelieving man? And how can she share her faith with him?

Unbelieving men, Peter advises, "may be won over without words by the behavior of their wives" (1 Peter 3:1). This is practical advice. No one ever was nagged into the kingdom. The most effective way for a Christian woman to win her husband to Christ is by consistently living the gospel in his presence over the long haul. Pure, reverent lives possess a strong persuasive power (v. 2).

---

church. If possible, it's good for other couples to visit in their home. Be hospitable, and remember to include the unchurched when you plan social events. Genuine hospitality (like an invitation for dinner or a barbecue) can provide nonthreatening opportunities for interaction and can build bridges for sharing the gospel.

4. Develop church programs that strengthen families. Sometimes the unchurched spouse may see church activities as a threat to his relationship with his wife. Sponsor marriage retreats, family emphasis weekends, or workshops on practical topics like child rearing or financial management. Make it clear that the church is family-friendly, and that a woman's commitment to Christ will make her a better wife, not worse.

5. Pray for them. Lift up the unsaved loved ones in prayer, and ask for God's wisdom and strength so that the Christian can set the right example.

Even when an unbelieving spouse remains unresponsive, God works through the Christian spouse to bring a valuable element of spiritual dignity and holy influence to the home. This can have a profound and lasting effect—especially on the children (see 1 Corinthians 7:14). For example, Timothy's father was a Greek, and the Scripture implies he was not a believer (Acts 16:1). But Timothy's grandmother, Lois, and his mom, Eunice, had a sincere faith living in them that rubbed off on Timothy from his earliest days (2 Timothy 1:5; 3:15).

When a Christian spouse responds to a non-Christian spouse with unselfish love, he or she is living out the grace of God—the kind of extra-abundant outpouring of grace Jesus referred to when he spoke about going the second mile and loving our enemies. God calls each member of the family to fulfill his or her own personal obligations, not to act as judge and jury over how well other family members are doing their parts.

As Richard W. DeHaan wrote, "You can 'I do' even if he doesn't."[3]

A LASTING KIND OF BEAUTY

First Peter 3:3 tells us where real beauty *doesn't* come. It doesn't spring from "outward adornment, such as braided hair and the wearing of gold jewelry and fine clothes." Some folk conclude that this verse completely prohibits wearing jewelry or attractive hairstyles of any kind. That is not Peter's intention, however, for the original Greek doesn't say "fine clothes," but simply "clothes." In other words, if you say this verse totally prohibits wearing jewelry or braided hair, by the same reasoning you'd have to conclude that it prohibits putting on any clothing at all![4] The point isn't that outward adornment is wrong. The point is that outward adornment isn't *enough*. We need to heed this instruction in a day when both men and women tend to be preoccupied with outward appearances. Just shampooing our hair is no longer enough. Now we add conditioner to make it soft, blow-dry it to add volume, mousse and spray it to hold it in place, then walk outdoors where one blast of wind can ruin the entire effect! Do we spend as much time and effort working on our inner beauty as we do on making the outside beautiful?

The word "adornment" (v. 3) is from the Greek *kosmos*, which is usually translated "world." This is where we get our word "cosmos" (an orderly arranged universe), and it's also the source of the word "cosmetics." There's nothing wrong with looking our best; in fact, care of the body is both a natural desire (Ephesians 5:29) and a Christian duty, especially since the Holy Spirit dwells in us (1 Corinthians 6:19, 20). But an attractive body without a healthy spirit is like a tasty-looking dessert that is all icing and no cake.

God warned the sinful women of Isaiah's day that the day would come when their fine clothes and jewelry would be snatched away from them (Isaiah 3:16-24). In Peter's day, people in Rome often tried to outdo one another with elaborate hairdos, studded with gold and silver combs and gaudy jewels. The satirist Juvenal (c. A.D. 60-140) associated extravagant clothing and makeup with marital unfaithfulness. He denounced the kind of Roman woman who "encircles her neck with green emeralds and fastens huge pearls to her elongated ears," and "puffs out and disfigures her face with lumps of dough" in a desperate attempt to improve the shape of her face.[5]

By contrast, Peter mentions several characteristics of the genuine beauty God desires in a Christian woman.

1. *Genuine beauty comes from the inner self.* Did you ever meet people who were eye-catchingly handsome or pretty on the outside, but when you talked with them awhile, you realized they were ugly or empty on the inside? Real beauty comes from the "inner self," the hidden person of the heart, not the facades we create to impress others. Like the unadvertised specials you sometimes encounter in a department store, some of the finest folk you'll ever meet are unspectacular on the outside but beautiful on the inside.

2. *Genuine beauty lasts.* Peter calls it "unfading beauty." The Greek word *aphthartos* ("unfading," or "incorruptible") is the same term Peter used earlier (1 Peter 1:4) to describe our unfading heavenly inheritance. A person's outward beauty often fades with the passing of time, but inner beauty increases as years go by. Marriages based mainly on physical attraction are headed for trouble unless the partners do a lot of maturing.

People who are considering marriage may look at their prospective partners and wonder, "What will he or she look like thirty years from now?" But a far more helpful question is, "Because of what I know about my prospective spouse's character, can I realistically expect him or her to grow more beautiful with the passing of time?"

3. *Genuine beauty is precious to God.* Outward appearances don't impress our creator, who looks upon our hearts (1 Samuel 16:7). God sees past our clothes, cosmetics, and carefully groomed exteriors. What he wants to see is "a gentle and quiet spirit" (1 Peter 3:4). "Gentle" (Greek *praus*) means "not insistent on one's own rights, not pushy, demanding, or selfishly assertive."[6] It's the same word Jesus used in the Beatitudes when he said, "Blessed are the meek." "Quiet" (Greek *hesuchiou*) is used to describe the way all Christians (both male and female) should strive to lead peaceful and quiet lives (1 Thessalonians 4:11; 1 Timothy 2:2), and it's the word Paul uses when he tells women to be "silent" or quiet in the church (1 Timothy 2:12). The truly beautiful woman knows how to control herself calmly; she doesn't need to flaunt her beauty or call unnecessary attention to herself. This kind of quiet, gentle, well-refined dignity is "of great worth in God's sight" (v. 4).

4. *Genuine beauty attracts people to Christ.* Remember, in the context of 1 Peter 3, Peter is talking about how women married to unbelievers can help lead their husbands to Christ. Will jewelry win a man to the Lord? Will fancy clothes, or perfect hair? No, but a beautiful spirit often proves irresistible.

Peter concludes his instructions to wives by pointing back to the beautiful "holy women of the past who put their hope in God" (v. 5). Women like Miriam, Deborah, Ruth, Esther, and Hannah come to mind. But Peter chooses to mention only one by name: Sarah, who serves as a great example of faith under fire.

Sarah joined her husband Abraham in packing up and moving from their home in Ur (Genesis 12:5). Twice she endured the indignity of being passed off as Abraham's sister (Genesis 12:11-20; 20:1-18). She became pregnant in her old age and gave birth to Isaac when she was ninety years old, then watched a few years later as Abraham marched off with the boy to Mount Moriah (Genesis 22:1-6). Surely she wondered what they were doing. Did she know that Abraham planned to sacrifice Isaac there on the mountain? Did she suspect that her faith would come under fire like this? It's an understatement to say that it wasn't easy to be Abraham's wife! (In fact, you could make a good argument that it probably was harder to be married to Abraham than to be married to Peter!)

Sarah wasn't perfect. She gave in to impatience and doubt and urged her husband to sleep with Hagar rather than trusting God to give her a child. Then she mistreated Hagar (Genesis 16:1-6). Later, she laughed when she heard God's promise that she would bear a son in her old age—then denied laughing when she was confronted (Genesis 18:9-15). It's encouraging that Scripture uses Sarah as a good example in spite of her human weaknesses. Her faith outshines her frailty. Today's godly women continue Sarah's legacy of faith when they "do what is right and do not give way to fear" (1 Peter 3:6).

HELPFUL WORDS FOR HUSBANDS

Peter uses six verses to talk about the role of the wives. Now he turns to the husbands with one forceful, thought-provoking sentence: "Husbands, in the same way be considerate as you live with your wives, and treat them with respect as the weaker partner and as heirs with you of the gracious gift of life, so that nothing will hinder your prayers" (v. 7).

Notice how Peter repeats the expression, "in the same way." He used the identical word (Greek *homoios*) to introduce his teaching about the role of the wives (v. 1). Both the wives and the husbands are to look back to the perfect example of Jesus Christ (2:21) and strive to live in humble submission "in the same way" the Lord did. How can a husband follow Jesus' footsteps in the home?

UNDERSTAND YOUR WIFE

Men often need to be reminded to "be considerate as you live with your wives," and "dwell with them according to knowledge" (*King James Version*), and live with them "in an understanding way" (*New*

American Standard Bible). Fellows, God is saying that marriage is one long process of education! We must not merely drift along, but be thoughtful and attentive, and spend time really thinking about our wife's unique personality, spiritual gifts, and needs.

My oldest child, Matt, was born in June. The following May my wife was privately excited to celebrate her first Mother's Day as a mom. She didn't communicate this to me, however, and in my ignorant insensitivity, it never occurred to me that I should give my wife a Mother's Day card or gift. After all, I reasoned, she isn't my mother—she's Matt's mother! I figured that when Matt was old enough to do so, he would give Candy a gift on Mother's Day.

When the big day arrived, I sent a Mother's Day card to my mom, but did nothing to honor my wife. Later that night, I couldn't figure out why my wife was giving me the "cold shoulder"—that is, until she explained her feelings of disappointment. My marriage education took a major leap forward that night!

Several years ago, Cecil Osborne wrote a book called *The Art of Understanding Your Mate*, in which he included "Ten Commandments for Husbands." I've paraphrased them as follows:

1. Treat your wife with gentle strength.
2. Encourage her with sincere words of praise and reassurance.
3. Clearly define the responsibilities each of you will perform individually, and those you will share together.
4. Avoid tearing her down with destructive criticism.
5. Remember the importance of "little things" (gifts, compliments, special dates) that express sensitivity and romance.
6. Make time for togetherness.
7. Build her sense of security.
8. Be patient with her during her emotional ups and downs, just as she must be with your own.
9. Cooperate with her every way you can to improve your marriage.
10. Discover her unique needs and try to meet them.[7]

The word translated "wives" in 1 Peter 3:7 is not the usual word for woman or wife. Used only here in the entire New Testament, the Greek word *gunaikeios* emphasizes the distinctive quality of femaleness;

it could be translated "feminine one." A husband must try to understand and appreciate his wife's uniqueness and femininity.

She's one of a kind—a priceless gift to be cherished.

RESPECT YOUR WIFE

Peter mentions two reasons a husband should respect his wife. First, she is "the weaker partner." Wait a minute—is this an insult to women? Another not-so-subtle indication of male chauvinism in the Bible?

No. Whatever "weakness" Peter means, it's not a reason for dishonor but for honor, not a cause for disrespect but for respect. The Bible often mentions women who proved themselves physically durable and spiritually tough (for example, Esther, Priscilla, and Phoebe). Peter's point here is not that the wife is so terribly weak, but that the husband must be so lovingly careful. Just as we would not be careless with a china cup we consider valuable, neither should we be harsh and reckless around our wives.

Does the phrase "weaker partner" refer to physical power? Anatomically, men have thicker skin, thicker skulls, and (in most cases, anyway) the strength to overpower their wives physically if they wanted to. Is Peter simply warning men to be tender and emotionally sensitive? Is he concerned that a woman's earnest efforts to submit, as taught in the first part of this chapter, will leave her vulnerable to mistreatment? Perhaps the best view is that men must avoid taking advantage of *any* kind of weakness they find in their wives.[8]

Here's another reason husbands must respect their wives: these godly women are "heirs with you of the gracious gift of life," of equal value in the eyes of God (1 Peter 3:7; see also Galatians 3:28). To mistreat your wife is to mistreat another child of God and risk having something "hinder your prayers" (1 Peter 3:7). The word "hinder" (Greek *ekkopto*) literally meant "to cut into," and was used for the way a tree was cut down when it bears no fruit (Matthew 3:10; 7:19; Luke 3:9). Marriage problems can cut into a person's prayer life and hinder our overall relationship with God.

A husband can show respect for his wife by the way he speaks to her, by the way he listens to her (genuinely hearing her concerns and valuing her opinions), and by the way he talks about her to others.

PRACTICAL WORDS FOR EVERYONE

No matter how hard we try, we'll still have some rough spots in our marriages. We are sinners, after all, who bring lots of "betrothal baggage" into our marriage relationships.

If we're to experience the abundant life Christ wants to give us, we may need to reverse some unhealthy habits that have been poisoning the atmosphere in our families.

Maybe you've heard the simple but thought-provoking illustration that "evil" is simply "live" in reverse. In other words, sin turns things around, reverses the proper order of things, and ruins God's best for our lives.

The fact is, "Whoever would love life and see good days must keep his tongue from evil and his lips from deceitful speech" (1 Peter 3:10).

Jesus will be more at home with us if we strive to develop a family atmosphere like the one described in 1 Peter 3:8-12; a family characterized by harmony, sympathy, brotherly love, compassion, and humility. Instead of looking for reasons to retaliate and point fingers, we can offer blessings and encouragement. We can "seek peace and pursue it" (v. 11).

What does it mean in a marriage to "seek peace and pursue it"? It means looking for and celebrating your mate's strengths, instead of focusing on his or her weaknesses. It means growing in Christ together, and looking for new ways to share the adventure of faith. It means laughing a lot, and refusing to allow joyless, worldly-minded people to determine your outlook on life. It means facing disagreements and working to resolve conflicts, being patient, and forbearing with one another in love. It means carefully protecting the respect you have for one another. It means choosing again and again to give up your own rights. It means confessing sin, and extending forgiveness. It means a deep unbending commitment to keep your vows. It means engaging in honest communication that leads to an ever-deepening oneness.

Many of these qualities aren't in our "betrothal baggage" when we start on our marital journeys. Together, we learn to pack spiritual qualities like these into our bags as we travel along.

If you find marriage a challenge, remember: God is there to help. Marriage is his idea, and if there's anyone pulling for us to make it, it's the Lord. He pays careful attention to our needs. Notice the vivid ways Peter describes the Lord's attentiveness: God's eyes are on the righteous; his ears hear our prayers; his face is against those who do evil (v. 12; see also Psalm 34:15, 16). The God of peace wants to be an active participant in your household.

Can you picture him standing at the door of your house, seeking entrance to your marriage, to your parenting, to your personal life?

Isn't it time you open the door and say, "Welcome to our home, Jesus"?

NOTES: CHAPTER FIVE

1. "Monogamy Underestimated?" *The Cincinnati Enquirer,* February 12, 1990.

2. I. Howard Marshall, *1 Peter* (Downers Grove, IL: InterVarsity, 1991), p. 98.

3. Richard W. DeHaan, *Good News for Bad Times* (Wheaton, IL: Victor Books, 1975), p. 69.

4. See Wayne Grudem, *1 Peter* (Grand Rapids: Eerdmans, 1988), p. 140.

5. Juvenal, *Satire* 6.457-65. See also J. Ramsey Michaels, *1 Peter* (Waco, Texas: Word, 1988), p. 159.

6. Grudem, p. 140.

7. Cecil G. Osborne, *The Art of Understanding Your Mate* (Grand Rapids: Zondervan, 1970), pp. 127-137.

8. Grudem, pp. 143, 144

CHAPTER SIX

No Longer Afraid

1 Peter 3:13-22; 4:1-11

Fear is an ugly word. Paradoxically, it's related to the Old English "fare" (to go). You pay a fare in order to travel on a train or plane. When people leave, you say "farewell," for you want them to enjoy a good and safe journey. Travel, though, has always been a dangerous thing. So with a tiny twist of spelling, the old word "fare" gave birth to another word, "fear," to describe something that poses a peril or an obstacle to the journey. Indeed, fear blocks progress. It keeps us from moving forward in faith.

Life is filled with perils. Many folk are afraid of natural disasters (like thunderstorms and earthquakes). Others fear crime (so they invest in security systems for their homes and cars). Some fear personal relationships and the commitment and potential conflicts they bring. Many would say that the ultimate cause for fear—and perhaps the root of all our other fears—is death. According to the Bible, Christ came to free those whom the devil has held in bondage to their fear of death (Hebrews 2:14, 15).

Some fears are well justified. They are natural responses to genuine danger. You're smart to be afraid of reckless drivers, dark alleys, volcanoes, drug dealers, and faulty brakes. Other fears are irrational—unhealthy phobias and unwarranted anxieties that paralyze, agonize, and immobilize us. Ironically, it's not unusual to find that Christians are afraid to talk about their faith with others—even though we possess the good news that Jesus came to set us free from fear and death.

The first mention of fear in the Bible is in Genesis 3:10, where

Adam told the Lord God, "I heard you in the garden, and I was afraid because I was naked; so I hid." Sometimes the Bible portrays fear as cowardice; for example, the Israelite soldiers who were afraid to fight Goliath (1 Samuel 17:11). Some fear is a response to a real or perceived threat, as was the case when Jesus' grief-stricken disciples hid behind locked doors in the upper room after the Lord was crucified (John 20:19). Sometimes Scripture also presents fear as a thoughtful response to the power and wisdom of God (Proverbs 1:7; Ecclesiastes 12:13). In this sense, it's even possible to "delight in the fear of the Lord" (Isaiah 11:2, 3). Someone has said, "The fear of God is the one fear that removes all others." His perfect love drives out fear (1 John 4:18, 19).

When Peter wrote his epistles, he was addressing people who struggled with fear. His first-century readers had good reasons to be anxious. They were vulnerable—threatened by official persecution by their government and misunderstanding by their neighbors. Peter's words to them served as a strong message of encouragement to a suffering church.

DON'T BE AFRAID TO SPEAK OUT

"Who is going to harm you if you are eager to do good? But even if you should suffer for what is right, you are blessed" (1 Peter 3:13, 14). As a general rule, doing what is right helps prevent many kinds of harm. For example, someone who obeys traffic laws is less likely to get into an accident than someone who drives recklessly. A person who avoids sexual immorality will also avoid sexually transmitted diseases. A person who pays her bills on time will avoid the harmful consequences of debt.

However, life is filled with examples of faithful people who suffered, even though they honestly served God and tried to do the right thing. Hebrews 11 tells about heroes of faith who conquered kingdoms and escaped from the sword, but it also tells about other equally faithful heroes who were tortured, stoned, sawed in two, and put to death by the sword (Hebrews 11:32-40). Skeptics sometimes theorize that faith in God is nothing but a crutch for the weak. Some crutch! A narrow path instead of the broad and easy way? Choosing to stand alone instead of blending in with the crowd? Jesus said to take up our cross and follow him. A cross is hardly a crutch. We do lean on God—but we also learn that the Lord's call to discipleship often includes a call to hardship. Faithful people will agree with the wise person who observed "Goodness is not always comfortable, and comfort is not always good."

We must not be afraid to speak out when our faith is under fire. Peter writes, "Do not fear what they fear; do not be frightened" (v. 14). Here Peter quotes loosely from Isaiah 8:12, 13, where the Lord instructed his people not to fear what faithless people fear. What makes unbelievers afraid? Losing things! If your life is wrapped up in earthly things, you'll be more afraid of losing your health, your money, your friends, and your respectability. While Christians do not enjoy losing such good things either, thankfully our life's purpose is not wrapped up in them. We have already counted everything as "loss for the sake of Christ" (Philippians 3:7). We've already decided to give up everything we have in order to be Jesus' disciples (Luke 14:33). So in an important sense, nothing really can be taken from us. We've already placed ourselves and our well-being into the Lord's hands. That's why we need to be neither *fearful* (Greek *phobos*) nor *frightened* (Greek *tarasso,* to be shaken up or emotionally upset, as King Herod was "disturbed" at the wise men's report in Matthew 2:3. Jesus said, "Do not let your hearts be troubled" (John 14:1). This was the same Lord who was calm enough to sleep during storms at sea (Mark 4:37, 38). Peter must have taken this lesson to heart. When Herod put him in prison, Peter was awaiting trial and probably execution, but, encouraged by his faith and uplifted by the church's prayers, Peter slept so soundly in the prison that the angel God sent to rescue him appears to have had a difficult time waking him up (Acts 12:1-7)! The peace of God reigned in Peter's heart and crowded out excessive fear.

Instead of being afraid, we must dare to publicly defend our faith when the opportunity presents itself. Here are five important reminders from 1 Peter 3:15, 16 for anyone who wants to speak out for Christ:

• *Before you speak to others, make sure Christ is Lord in your own heart.* "But in your hearts set apart Christ as Lord." Our goal is not just to win arguments, but to honor our Lord and to help precious people find the Savior.

• *Be prepared at all times.* "Always be prepared to give an answer." You never know when you'll get a chance to share your faith. Make sure you know what you believe and why. Prepare yourself in advance through study and prayer so you'll have something worthwhile to say. "Be prepared in season and out of season" (2 Timothy 4:2), because a helpful word of witness never goes out of season.

• *Offer reasonable answers to honest questions.* "Give an answer to everyone who asks you." Peter not only tells us to offer answers and reasons (the Greek word is *apologia,* which means a reasonable defense or explanation); he also assumes that people will ask us about our faith. Our lives must be noticeably different so that others will be curious. If we're acting like the salt of the earth, we'll make people thirsty.

• *Emphasize hope.* Notice: unbelievers will ask you to give "the reason for the hope that you have." Genuine intellectual questions need to be answered thoughtfully and seriously. But the fact is, often people outside of Christ aren't too interested in our philosophical arguments or our theological debates. They may have no interest at all in discussing the conflicting views of various religious denominations. But you can be sure, your non-Christian friends are searching for hope. People outside of Christ are "without hope and without God in the world" (Ephesians 2:12). It's hard—perhaps impossible—to live every day without hope. If you've experienced the new birth "into a living hope" (1 Peter 1:3), you have something priceless to share.

• *Speak out with gentleness and respect.* Peter says to give reasons for our faith, "but do this with gentleness and respect." In other words, we can be bold without being brutal, helpful without being hateful, courageous without being crude. Many folk have been turned off by harsh, angry encounters with well-meaning but ill-tempered Christians who left the false impression that righteousness and rudeness usually go together. A gospel of grace must be defended graciously. Too many times, instead of providing clear, respectful answers, Christians blow people away with a quarrelsome approach. "As charcoal to embers and as wood to fire, so is a quarrelsome man for kindling strife" (Proverbs 26:21).

Paul warned Timothy, "Don't have anything to do with foolish and stupid arguments, because you know they produce quarrels. And the Lord's servant must not quarrel; instead, he must be kind to everyone, able to teach, not resentful" (2 Timothy 2:23, 24). Even when you strongly disagree with another person's point of view, you can treat him with respect and give his ideas a fair hearing. Then your own conscience will be clear, and your example untarnished. You'll be "keeping a clear conscience, so that those who speak maliciously against your good behavior in Christ may be ashamed of their slander" (v. 16).

It's interesting to remember that there once was a time when Peter himself failed to live up to this teaching. A servant girl asked him about his relationship with Jesus Christ, and Peter was unprepared and unwilling to answer. He denied Jesus, not once, but three times that night (Matthew 26:69-75)—a painful failure that doubtlessly burned its way deeply into Peter's memory. After Jesus rose from the dead and the Holy Spirit came, however, Peter was not afraid to speak out; he could do nothing other than speak boldly for his Lord. He said, "We cannot help speaking about what we have seen and heard" (Acts 4:20).

DON'T BE AFRAID TO STAND OUT

First Peter 3:17-22 has been called one of the most difficult passages to interpret in the entire New Testament. Space will not allow a thorough treatment of the many questions that arise.[1] We shouldn't be deterred, though, from learning the encouraging lessons that Peter clearly intended his readers to understand.

JESUS STANDS OUT

Christians can take courage in times of suffering because of the unique work of Christ our Lord. Some of the details may seem somewhat puzzling in these verses, but the overall message is powerful and clear.

• *Jesus stands out because he "died for sins once for all" (v. 18).* No imperfect human leader ever could do what Christ alone did for us. He paid sin's penalty to bring us to God. He was willing to make himself vulnerable (from the Latin *vulnus,* "wound") as a sacrifice for sin. It helps us feel less vulnerable ourselves when we remember that we serve a "woundable Lord" who was willing to make himself vulnerable and share our hurts.

• *Jesus stands out because of his power in the realm of the Spirit.* Through the Spirit, Christ "went and preached to the spirits in prison" (vv. 18, 19). Long standing church tradition understands this to mean that between his death on the cross and his resurrection on the first day of the week, Christ proclaimed his completed messianic work in the realm of the dead—perhaps to the old covenant saints who had been awaiting his coming, or to the fallen angels who disobeyed God during Satan's original rebellion. Another view is that through the Spirit-inspired preaching of Noah, Christ proclaimed repentance to those "who disobeyed long ago when God waited patiently in the days of Noah while the ark was being built" (v. 20). In any case, Peter's point is that Christ reigns in power in the spiritual realm.

• *Jesus stands out because he rose from the dead.* The resurrection of Jesus is both a fact of history and an indispensable part of our personal salvation. The water of the Genesis flood "symbolizes baptism that now saves you also—not the removal of dirt from the body but the pledge of a good conscience toward God. It saves you by the resurrection of Jesus Christ" (v. 21).

Peter has no problem mentioning baptism in connection with salvation. After all, he's the same apostle who told all his listeners on the Day of Pentecost to "repent and be baptized" (Acts 2:38; see also Matthew 28:18-20; Mark 16:16; Acts 16:15, 33; 18:8). Peter is careful not to leave the impression that baptism is some sort of an empty outward ritual, a mere ceremonial dipping in the water. Without faith and repentance, baptism loses its biblical meaning. Without the grace of God and the work of Christ accomplished on the cross, baptism loses its biblical meaning. But when a sincere believer accepts God's grace with humility and eagerness, baptism becomes "the pledge of a good conscience toward God" (v. 21). It's a joyful event people enthusiastically ask for, instead of argue against.

It's sad to me that today's Christian world often treats baptism as a point of theological controversy and debate. In the Bible, baptism is a joyful expression of personal faith and a point of commonality and unity with the rest of the church—something we share in common with other believers (like the other "ones" mentioned in Ephesians 4:1-6). And from my experiences in bringing people to Christ, I've observed that when folk begin to grasp the love of God and the wonder of his grace, baptism isn't a cause for controversy but for commitment and joy. We need to encourage new believers to welcome baptism with the kind of eager attitude the Ethiopian expressed when he requested the privilege of being baptized (Acts 8:36).

A believer's baptism is inextricably tied to the death and resurrection of Christ (Romans 6:1-4; Colossians 2:12).[2] If Jesus didn't rise from the

---

HOW STRANGE ARE YOU?

When Peter says unbelievers think Christians are "strange" (1 Peter 4:4), he uses an interesting word. The verb *xenizo* and its noun form *xenos* sometimes mean "alien or foreign" (as in Acts 17:18, 21; Ephesians 2:19; Hebrews 11:13). Oddly, these terms sometimes are translated "to entertain, lodge, or provide hospitality" (as in Acts 10:23; Hebrews 13:2; 3 John 5).

In other words, *xenos* has a twofold connotation. It could mean that a person seems strange or foreign to you, but it could also express your willingness to welcome the stranger into your home. (There's a similar irony in the way "host," one who receives guests, is from the same Latin root *hostis* as the word "hostile.")

Unbelievers may feel that Christians are strange, different, a little unsettling or uncomfortable to be around. At the same time, they may find us strangely appealing because they are attracted to the Lord we serve. This "strangeness" on the part of Christians can actually be used by God to draw others to Christ. It's not that Christians are weird. It's just that the Spirit's presence living in us should make us obviously, and appealingly, different. It pays to be "peculiar people"!

---

dead, not only is baptism meaningless, our very life and faith are point-less as well. In the midst of a world gripped by fear and death, how wonderful it is to know that Christ did indeed rise from the dead, and that we can be united with him in his victory (1 Corinthians 15:17-20)!

• *Jesus stands out because he "has gone into Heaven and is at God's right hand"* (v. 22). Jesus' ascension is described in Luke 24:50, 51, and in Acts 1:6-11. The significance of his ascension is described in passages like Romans 8:31-39 and Hebrews 1:1-4. Why should we be afraid? Our master reigns in Heaven. He's "got the whole world in his hands." Even "angels, authorities, and powers" are in submission to him (v. 22).

WE STAND OUT

Not only does Jesus Christ stand out, but, in a sense, so do his fol-lowers. We stand out "like stars in the universe" when we live in accor-dance with God's life-giving Word (Philippians 2:15, 16).

Two approaches to life are described in 1 Peter 4:1-6. One very pop-ular (but destructive) way is to devote yourself to "evil human desires." The better way is to live "for the will of God" (v. 2).

If you choose to follow God's will, you'll stand out like a light in a dark place. If you choose to ignore God, you'll experience several nega-tive consequences:

• *You will waste your time.* "You have spent enough time in the past doing what pagans choose to do" (v. 3).

• *You may spoil your physical health.* Sins like "debauchery, lust, drunkenness, orgies, carousing" (v. 3) often lead to injury, illness, fami-ly problems, arrest, and even death. Without God, many fall into what Peter calls a "flood of dissipation" (v. 4). The word for flood (Greek *anachusin*) refers to an outpouring or steady flow—a vivid way to por-tray the temporarily exciting, but ultimately unsatisfying, pursuit of pleasure. It's like riding a raft down a swiftly flowing stream toward a giant waterfall; it's a fun, wild ride for a while, but then comes destruc-tion. "Dissipation" (Greek *asotia*) refers to squandering one's life or resources, an extravagant wastefulness. Paul used this word in Ephesians 5:18, for example, when he urged, "Do not get drunk on wine, which leads to debauchery." The Christian life is concentrated, focused, purposeful; the non-Christian life is dissipated, unfocused, lacking a goal or a guide.

• *You will insult God.* False worship and a sinful lifestyle are not merely minor offenses to shrug off. Peter calls this kind of thing "detestable idolatry" (v. 3).

When you turn to Christ, non-Christians—even some of your old friends—may not understand your new commitment. They may think it's strange that your life is changing. They may not understand why you don't join in their sin, and they may even "heap abuse on you" (v. 4). Better to be insulted for doing what's right than to do things that insult the Lord.

• *You will eventually face God's judgment.* Everyone, including those who belittle Christians, must someday "give account to him who is ready to judge the living and the dead" (v. 5).

DON'T BE AFRAID TO STEP OUT

Because Jesus is our Lord, and his powerful Spirit dwells in us, we don't need to be afraid to speak out, to stand out, or to step out.

STEP OUT AND PRAY BOLDLY

Peter says to "be clear minded and self-controlled so that you can pray" (v. 7). The word for "clear minded" (Greek *sophronein*) literally meant to be in one's right mind, in control of oneself, or sane. It was used to describe the new mental health enjoyed by a man Jesus healed of demon-possession (Mark 5:15). Paul used the term in contrast with being "beside oneself" or "mad" (2 Corinthians 5:13) and in contrast to "thinking too highly of oneself" (Romans 12:3). Prayer helps keep our minds clear. It is part of God's prescription for good mental health, and a vital way to overcome fear. In prayer we find courage to step out, even when our faith is under fire.

STEP OUT AND LOVE BOLDLY

"Love each other deeply," Peter says (v. 8). The word translated "deeply" (Greek *ektene*) literally meant "stretched out" or "strained." It brings to mind an athlete stretching out to make a play, like an outfielder in a baseball game who strains to reach a fly ball. The Greeks used this word to describe the way a horse stretched to reach its top speed. Love isn't always an easy, comfortable, "natural" thing to do. It often requires a strenuous effort. Love stretches us. We are to love one another "strenuously" or earnestly, not being afraid to risk or sacrifice. This kind of love is far more than an emotional feeling; it's a decision to act in the best interests of others no matter what the cost.

This kind of bold, fearless love "covers over a multitude of sins" (v. 8). This doesn't mean we ignore or condone sin. But love seeks to "cover" and forgive sin, not merely to expose and condemn it. Sometimes we must confront sin head-on, but never merely to point fingers of accusation and say, "Look what he did!" Through the blood of Christ, God's love covers our own multitude of sins. Likewise, God's love compels us to take the most gracious actions we can toward others. Love "keeps no record of wrongs." It "does not delight in evil but rejoices with the truth" (1 Corinthians 13:5, 6).

One way we can step out in love is by opening our homes to others. "Offer hospitality to one another without grumbling" (v. 9). By exercising hospitality, we can turn our homes into "hospitals"—places of healing and rest. And we're not to complain about the inconvenience. Be hospitable, Peter urges, "without grumbling." "Grumbling" (Greek *goggusmou*) is probably an example of onomatopoeia (a word that sounds like what it describes). Too often, there's a lot of "goggusmou-ing" going on in our hearts as we serve others. Perhaps we could paraphrase this verse, "Be hospitable to each other without griping about it or secretly wishing you didn't have to be!"

STEP OUT AND USE YOUR GIFTS BOLDLY

"Each one should use whatever gift he has received to serve others" (v. 10). Every Christian has received a gift or gifts from God, who is the giver of every good and perfect gift (see James 1:17). And if God has given you a gift, his purpose is not for you to show it off, but for you to use it "to serve others," thus "faithfully administering God's grace in its various forms" (v. 10).

"Various forms" translates the Greek *poikiles,* which means "variegat-ed" or "multicolored." We shouldn't picture Christ's church as gray and dull—a blah, bland, boring body where everyone looks and acts exactly the same. God's many-faceted grace is multicolored—it takes many forms as individual believers exercise their gifts.

I love small children, but teaching them in Sunday school isn't my strength. I admire the work of skillful artists, but I can barely draw a stick-person myself. I enjoy good music, but you don't want to hear my terrible trombone toots. God has filled his church with a colorful, diversified assortment of people with different God-given abilities who all serve the same Lord. Some believers are gifted speakers; if so, they must be careful to say only what is true to the Bible, "speaking the very words of God" (v. 11). Others are not public speakers; they must be careful to minister through deeds of service "with the strength God provides" (v. 11). No matter what gifts we use, the goal is that "in all things God may be praised through Jesus Christ" so that he will receive "the glory and the power for ever and ever" (v. 11).

As you read through the Bible, notice how many times you see the words, "Do not be afraid." From the angel who announced Jesus' birth (Luke 2:10) to the angel who told the women about Jesus' resurrec-tion (Matthew 28:5), a theme of victory over fear runs throughout the life of Christ.

He can help you speak out, stand out, and step out—even when your faith is under fire.

Don't be afraid.

NOTES: CHAPTER SIX

1. For a readable explanation of several different points of view about this passage, see Wayne Grudem, *1 Peter* (Grand Rapids: Eerdmans, 1988), pp. 203-220. Grudem argues in favor of the view that Peter's intended meaning likely focuses on the Spirit of Christ preaching through Noah in the years prior to the flood. See also Raymond C. Kelcy, *The Letters of Peter and Jude* (Austin, TX: R. B. Sweet Co., 1972), pp. 75-80.

2. This helps to explain the significance of baptism by immersion, in which a believer is buried in water and raised up from the water, just as Jesus was buried and raised up from his tomb in the earth.

CHAPTER SEVEN

The View Through Tear-Filled Eyes

1 Peter 4:12-19

Have you ever wondered why God allows evil and suffering to exist? If so, you are not alone. Everyone wonders about it sometimes . . . during tense moments in hospital emergency rooms while you're waiting for word about a loved one's condition . . . when you read yet another newspaper report about a terrorist bombing that claimed dozens of lives . . . when you're standing in line at a funeral home with a group of grief-stricken mourners. It's a question that pops up in youth groups as well as in nursing homes—a question many people wrestle with during troubling moments of private doubt. Why is there so much suffering in the world?

Skeptics often use this question as a reason to deny the existence of God altogether. Others see this question, not as a challenge to the *existence* of God, but as a challenge to the *character* of God. They suggest that, if there is a God, he must be toying with us, tormenting us, watching our misery with glee. They agree with Shakespeare's line in *King Lear,* "As flies to wanton boys, are we to the gods; They kill us for their sport."

Twentieth-century writer and philosopher H. L. Mencken wrote:

> The act of worship, as carried on by Christians, seems to me to be debasing rather than ennobling. It involves groveling before a Being who, if He really exists, deserves to be denounced instead of respected. I see little evidence in this world of the so-called goodness of God. On the contrary, on the strength of His daily acts, He must be set down a most stupid, cruel, and villainous fellow. . . . I simply can't imagine revering the God of war and politics, theology and cancer.[1]

Ordinary people say it this way: "If there is a God, then why are there wars? Why is there senseless killing? Why did God allow millions to die in the cruel Holocaust? Why does he allow babies to be born deformed or retarded? Why do accidents happen that cause innocent people to suffer? Why are there natural disasters like earthquakes, tornadoes, and hurricanes?"

During my college years I talked at length with a sociology professor who considered himself an unbeliever, although he had been brought up as a Roman Catholic. He was a well-educated man, with a Ph.D. from Notre Dame, but filled with sadness and despair that he attributed to a drinking problem and a failed marriage. One day, as I met with him in his office, he leaned forward in his chair, peered at me across his desk, and asked, "Why do you believe in God?" This was a rather intimidating situation for me—a twenty-one-year-old college student at the time. But I explained, as best I could, my reasons for believing in Christ and the Bible. When I finished, the professor looked at me and said, "Sometimes I wish I could believe as you do. But if there is a God, can you explain to me why innocent people die on the highways? Why does a semitrailer jump the guardrail and kill a mother and her young children? Why do terrible things like that happen, if God exists and God is good?"

I didn't know what to say. The old professor was asking a tough, age-old question. Philosophers frame it this way: If God is good and loving, he could destroy evil.

And, we reason, if God is all-powerful, he would destroy evil. Yet evil clearly exists—so maybe God isn't good, or isn't powerful, or doesn't exist at all. As one witty cynic phrased it, "What's a nice God like you doing in a universe like this?"

People we encounter in the pages of Scripture asked these questions too. Does life seem unfair? So it seemed to Solomon:

> I have seen something else under the sun: The race is not to the swift or the battle to the strong, nor does food come to the wise or wealth to the brilliant or favor to the learned; but time and chance happen to them all. Moreover, no man knows when his hour will come: As fish are caught in a cruel net, or birds are taken in a snare, so men are trapped by evil times that fall unexpectedly upon them.   Ecclesiastes 9:11, 12

Do you ever look around and see injustice and pain, and wonder why God doesn't intervene? Listen to Habakkuk:

> How long, O Lord, must I call for help, but you do not listen? Or cry out to you, "Violence!" but you do not save? Why do you make me look at injustice? Why do you tolerate wrong? Destruction and violence are before me; there is strife, and conflict abounds. Therefore the law is paralyzed, and justice never prevails. The wicked hem in the righteous, so that justice is perverted.
>
> Habakkuk 1:2-4

In a time of great pain, even the great King David felt abandoned by God and exclaimed:

> My God, my God, why have you forsaken me? Why are you so far from saving me, so far from the words of my groaning? O my God, I cry out by day, but you do not answer, by night, and am not silent.   Psalm 22:1, 2

And in his vision of Heaven, the apostle John saw the martyred saints under the altar crying out, "How long, Sovereign Lord, holy and true, until you judge the inhabitants of the earth and avenge our blood?" (Revelation 6:10).

In June 1988 a businessman from North Carolina was sleeping quietly in his room at the Helmsley Palace Hotel in New York City. Unknown to the hotel employees, a leaky roof had weakened the ceiling in the man's room. Suddenly a large section of plaster gave way and collapsed, killing the man in his bed below.

In March 1994 a tornado plowed through the town of Piedmont, Alabama, and the area nearby on a Palm Sunday morning and killed dozens of people—including nineteen people who were worshiping in a church facility that lay in the path of the storm.

On July 17, 1996, TWA flight 800 exploded a few minutes after takeoff, killing all 230 people on board. While boats, cranes, and FBI agents searched the debris for causes, the rest of us searched for answers.

We can't help but ask, "Why? Why those people? Why that moment?" There are no easy answers. But it's reassuring to see that the Bible doesn't dodge these hard questions. The problem is in reconciling statements like these: God is good. Evil exists. God is all-powerful.

All three are consistent with the teachings of Scripture. We would diagram it like this:

GOD IS GOOD   **GOD IS ALL-POWERFUL**

EVIL EXISTS

The Bible doesn't fall into the errors of the Christian Science sect, which holds that evil is an illusion. Nor does the Scripture minimize the problem, as if our pain is no big deal. One lengthy portion of Scripture (the book of Job) is devoted to an in-depth, realistic exploration of the problem of evil and suffering.

In a sense, the book of 1 Peter presents a brief but hopeful New Testament response to the hard questions of Job. Peter—no stranger to suffering himself—offers powerful and practical guidance for sufferers in 1 Peter 4:12-19.

DON'T BE SURPRISED BY SUFFERING

"Dear friends, do not be surprised at the painful trial you are suffering, as though something strange were happening to you" (v. 12). As someone wisely pointed out, "To be surprised at suffering is to be surprised that one of Jesus' predictions actually came true." Jesus was bluntly honest about the likelihood of experiencing pain. He combined realism with hope when he said, "In this world you will have trouble [or tribulation, *KJV*]. But take heart! I have overcome the world" (John 16:33).

The apostle Paul suffered hunger, thirst, beatings, shipwrecks, stonings, and almost constant harassment from his opponents. He saw suffering, not only as a consequence of living in a sin-tarnished, "groaning" planet, but also as a blessed privilege commonly experienced by those who choose to follow Christ (Romans 8:18-22; 2 Corinthians 11:23-28; Philippians 1:29; 2 Timothy 3:12). It would be nice if every new Christian emerged from baptism wearing a special space suit to ward off all pain and discomfort—but that's not the way Paul saw it.

Wayne Smith, who preached for years at Southland Christian Church in Lexington, Kentucky, said it's like a person who goes to the blood bank, then walks out complaining, "You know what they did to me in there? You won't believe it! *They took some of my blood!*" Of course they did—that's what happens when you visit a blood bank. According to Wayne, when you visit the dentist, you aren't shocked when he drills or even pulls out one of your teeth—that's what happens in dentists' offices! Likewise, we shouldn't be shocked when we encounter suffering and hardship in this world. If the Bible is to be believed at all, we must expect to face suffering as part of life on this fallen earth.

DON'T BE SURPRISED BY THE VARIETY OF FORMS OF SUFFERING

All suffering is not alike. It can take many forms. Remember what Peter wrote in 1 Peter 1:6? We face "all kinds of trials." Some of us must endure intense physical pain. The Greek word translated "painful trial" in 1 Peter 4:12 is *purosis,* the word for fire. (It's where we get our term "pyromaniac," someone who has an irresistible urge to set fires.) Some see in this verse a reference to the way the evil Emperor Nero had Christians rolled in pitch, put up on poles, and set on fire as living torches to light his gardens at night. We can be sure that the early believers read Peter's epistle with interest in times of intense persecution, when an open confession of faith could well mean being thrown to wild beasts, burned at the stake, or killed with a sword. To them, "faith under fire" was an all-too-literal possibility.

Some suffering takes a less tangible form: there are emotional pains and inner griefs that no external medicine or salve can heal. Peter's first-century readers evidently faced the indignity of social abuse. They were insulted, unfairly criticized, and publicly ridiculed. (Notice how many times 1 Peter alludes to this kind of verbal persecution: 1 Peter 2:12, 15; 3:16; 4:4, 14.) If you have ever been the target of critical or unfounded accusations, you understand the pain such slander can cause.

Abraham Lincoln was the object of unrelenting criticism throughout much of his career. His response? "I have endured a great deal of ridicule without much malice, and have received a great deal of kindness, not quite free of ridicule. I am used to it."

Another time he said, "If I were to read, much less answer, all the attacks made on me, this shop might as well be closed. . . . I can do the best I know how—the very best I can, and I mean to keep doing so until the end. If the end brings me out all right, what is said against me won't amount to anything. If the end brings me out wrong, ten angels swearing I was right would make no difference."

Maybe you have been spared intense physical pain. Perhaps you have never known the inner agony of deep depression or relentless grief. Never minimize the suffering of others just because their pain is different from your own. Hurts come in many different varieties. Someone has said, "Minor surgery is someone else's surgery." Somehow, no surgical procedure seems minor if it's being performed on you!

Lincoln once commented, "Whenever I hear anyone arguing for slavery, I feel a strong impulse to see it tried on him personally."

It's interesting that Peter uses a form of the same word (*poikeles*, manifold, variegated, many-colored) to describe both the trials Christians face and the grace God gives to his people (1:6; 4:10). Trials come in many forms, but there is grace from God to meet every challenge.

LEARN TO REJOICE IN SUFFERING

Do you ever feel overwhelmed? If you're a student, you probably feel overwhelmed when final exams, research papers, and other assignments all seem to be due at the same time. One of my friends told me that medical school is like putting your mouth at the end of a fire hose, and every day, the professors just keep pouring in more and more water. It's too much to take in, and no one ever shuts off the water!

New parents can feel overwhelmed. There are so many changes to make—and we're not just talking about diapers. Having children takes a tremendous amount of time, money, and energy.

Just the everyday demands of life can make us feel overwhelmed—
or at least "whelmed." The dictionary says "whelm" is a verb meaning
"to turn upside down" (like a capsized ship), "to cover or engulf, usually with disastrous effects." Being overwhelmed must be *really* bad,
since simply being whelmed is bad enough!

Here's are a few sure ways to feel overwhelmed: spend a day walking with a police officer on his beat, or with a social worker or a counselor. Visit a Third World country where poverty weighs down the people like a never-ending blanket of gloom.

And yet . . . I know Christian police officers and social workers who
make it through their days with a positive attitude. I have a friend
who works as a pastoral counselor and listens to other people's problems all day; yet he does his work with cheerfulness and sees it as a
way to serve Christ. I have friends who are serving as missionaries in
Ethiopia; somehow they serve the Lord with effectiveness and good
humor even in the midst of overwhelming physical and spiritual
needs. I've visited hospital patients who were suffering intense pain,
yet by the time I left they had made me feel more cheerful than when
I arrived. In the extreme poverty of Port-au-Prince, Haiti, I met some
of the most dedicated and joy-filled Christians I've ever known.

What's going on in these folk's lives? How are they able to
encounter overwhelming circumstances—and endure intense hardships—with an attitude of faith and joy?

They have learned that there is fellowship with Christ in times of
suffering. Peter writes that you can "rejoice that you participate in the
sufferings of Christ, so that you may be overjoyed when his glory is
revealed" (v. 13). It doesn't say *when* God's glory will be revealed.
While it's natural to see this verse as a reference to the glory of Christ's
second coming, it's also true that God's glory can be revealed in us
throughout life as we honor him. This is true even in times of hardship, when our faith is under fire.

When Jesus encountered a man blind from birth, the disciples
wanted to know why such an act of suffering could occur. They asked,
"Who sinned, this man or his parents, that he was born blind?" Like
most of us, the disciples figured that you had to be able to definitely

pin the blame on someone. But Jesus wouldn't oversimplify this situation by assigning blame or delving into a deep philosophical explanation. He simply stated, "Neither this man nor his parents sinned, but this happened so that the work of God might be displayed in his life" (John 9:1-3). Later the man was healed, and served as living testimony that Jesus is indeed "the light of the world" just as he claimed to be.

Likewise, when Jesus' friend Lazarus was sick, the disciples must have been quite puzzled at first by Jesus' statement, "This sickness will not end in death." Lazarus did die—only later did the disciples realize how, just as Jesus said, Lazarus' sickness didn't end in death because death itself wasn't the end for Lazarus! As hard as it was for Mary, Martha, and the others to comprehend, all of this was "for God's glory so that God's Son may be glorified through it" (John 11:4). We can catch a glimpse of joy in any situation when we recognize that somehow God will be glorified in it.

In the midst of our hardships, however, it's hard to see anything glorious. I remember one particularly gloomy day during my ten-year ministry in New York. I was feeling discouraged as I steered my car through heavy traffic. Dark late-afternoon thunderclouds loomed overhead, and my mood matched the weather. I turned on my windshield wipers as a light rain began to fall, and I inched my car onto an exit ramp. That's when I saw the rainbow—not one, but two—double arcs of vivid color displayed in the eastern sky. Apparently the rainbows had been there all along, but I had been looking the wrong direction. Preoccupied with my problems and pressures, I had nearly missed a beautiful reminder of God's faithfulness.

Sometimes Christians become so downhearted we miss our everyday "Immanuel Moments," those startling little reminders that God truly is with us. God is always present with his people, but he is a "very present help in trouble" (Psalm 46:1, KJV).

We can rejoice not only because there is a special kind of fellowship with Christ in our times of suffering, but also because, as Peter reminds us, suffering for righteousness' sake will be rewarded. "If you are insulted because of the name of Christ, you are blessed" (1 Peter 4:14). How are we blessed? Suffering can build our character (James

1:2-4). Suffering can help build the unity of the church, as believers come to one another's aid in Christian love (1 Corinthians 12:26). Suffering blesses us by reminding us of our need for God's help—in the words of C. S. Lewis, pain can be "God's megaphone to rouse a deaf world."

But frankly, no matter how much we talk about the "blessings" of suffering, pain still hurts! When we speak of rejoicing during times of suffering, we're not saying that Christians are masochists. It's just that even in the midst of the hurts, God can give us a peace that passes understanding. As someone has said, "Pain is inevitable, but misery is optional." When Christians choose joy instead of misery, this joy isn't something we conjure up on our own. It comes from the Holy Spirit, who even takes our painful groanings before the throne of God (Romans 8:26, 27).

According to Peter, that's why you can consider yourself blessed even during a time when you're suffering insults for Jesus' sake. "The Spirit of glory and of God rests on you," Peter says (1 Peter 1:14). The same Greek word for "rest" (*anapauo*) appears in Matthew 11:28, where Jesus says, "Come to me . . . and I will give you *rest*," in Mark 6:31, where the Lord told his disciples to "come with me by yourselves to a quiet place and get some *rest,*" and in Philemon 20, where Paul urged Philemon, "*refresh* my heart in Christ." The Holy Spirit is at home with us, still comfortable living in us, even when we're hurting. He is our source of refreshment, renewal, and strength.

BE CAREFUL TO AVOID DESERVED SUFFERING

Though our first inclination often is to blame God for our troubles, the fact is, much human suffering results from the abuse of our own free will. Proverbs 19:3 accurately observes, "A man's own folly ruins his life, yet his heart rages against the Lord."

According to philosopher and apologist Norman Geisler, God "created the fact of freedom; we perform the acts of freedom."[2] Further, Geisler argues, God "is not responsible for what people do with their freedom any more than automobile manufacturers are responsible for all the accidents resulting from reckless driving."[3] This is part of the answer to the dilemma presented at the beginning of this chapter: if God is loving and all-powerful, why does evil exist? It's precisely because God is loving that he voluntarily restrains his own power at times in order to achieve a higher good. He is all-powerful (omnipotent), but his power includes the power of self-control! God is not just raw power out of control. In the words of C. S. Lewis, he has granted human beings the "dignity of causality," the privilege of real involvement in the outcome of events.

Thus, a person who drinks too much shouldn't blame God for the pounding head and nausea of his hangover. One who eats too much shouldn't blame God for his indigestion and excess weight. The person who engages in premarital or extramarital sex shouldn't blame God when an unplanned pregnancy occurs. The spouse abuser shouldn't blame God for his wrecked marriage. The heavy smoker is hypocritical if he tries to blame God for his lung cancer. Much suffering simply results from our own foolish or sinful choices. We reap what we sow (Galatians 6:7, 8).

So Peter urges, "If you suffer, it should not be as a murderer or thief or any other kind of criminal, or even as a meddler" (v. 15). In other words, "Don't do things that make you deserve to suffer." We're just asking for trouble if we kill, steal, or meddle in others' business.

Of course, not all suffering can be explained this way. Some of the most perplexing and heartbreaking examples of suffering occur when a seemingly innocent person is afflicted with pain. What about babies who suffer and die from disease? What about the toddlers who died when wicked King Herod slaughtered the innocents (Matthew 2:16)? What about the many who, through no fault of their own, suffer at the hands of evil tyrants like Adolf Hitler or Saddam Hussein?

Several years ago, my father-in-law was mugged and severely beaten by an unknown assailant who accosted him outside a motel room. My father-in-law has been a faithful preacher of God's Word for years. The emotional terror and physical bruises he endured were the result of his attacker's sin, not his own.

Baseball player Dave Dravecky lost his pitching arm to cancer. He is a dedicated Christian. Obviously, bad things do happen to good people. Part of the answer lies in the risks associated with human freedom. The same interdependence of human life that provides opportunities to love, to give, and to serve, also makes it possible for people to hate, to take, and to harm. The sins of a person in power—even the sins of a previous generation—can bring pain and hardship to others. But there is an important limitation to this: someone else's sin can cause you to suffer, but cannot cause you to lose your soul. Each of us is personally accountable to God (Ezekiel 18:20).

ACCEPT THE LIKELIHOOD OF SUFFERING AS A CHRISTIAN

"If you suffer as a Christian, do not be ashamed, but praise God that you bear that name" (v. 16). Though the name is quite common today, the title "Christian" appears only three times in the New Testament. The other two occurrences are in Acts 11:26 (where the disciples were "called Christians first at Antioch") and in Acts 26:28 (where Agrippa told Paul he was "almost persuaded" to be a Christian).

Come to think of it, it's only natural that a Christ-follower should suffer. After all, Christ himself was called "Beelzebub" (a Jewish name for Satan) by his enemies; so Christ's followers shouldn't be surprised when we receive similar treatment (see Matthew 10:24, 25). God himself is well-acquainted with innocent suffering; he experienced it himself!

People say, "Why doesn't God destroy evil? If he loves us, why doesn't he step in and intervene? Why doesn't he do something to save us?" Then we open the New Testament, and the answer hits us right in the face: God *has done something*—the greatest thing! He has come to earth, lived among us in the person of his Son, experienced unimaginable suffering . . . then conquered death by rising from the grave. We will not experience the full and final benefits of Christ's victory until he returns at the end of time. Nevertheless, his triumph and our comfort are assured.

When a distraught woman asked J. W. McGarvey, "Where was your God when my son died?" the preacher answered, "The same place he was when his *own* Son died."

FOCUS ON THE QUESTIONS YOU CAN ANSWER

Sometimes it isn't a cop-out to say simply, "I don't know." Sometimes suffering is nearly impossible to explain. Deuteronomy 29:29 is a helpful verse. It reminds us, "The secret things belong to the Lord our God, but the things revealed belong to us and to our children forever,

---

WHAT CAUSES SUFFERING?

The following chart summarizes some of what we know about the various causes of suffering.

1. Some suffering is the direct result of my own sinful choices (Galatians 6:7, 8).

2. Some suffering is the result of sins committed by others (Matthew 2:16; Genesis 4:8; 2 Samuel 11:14-17).

3. Some suffering results from natural laws that sometimes bring harm in a world tainted by sin (Genesis 3:17-19; Romans 8:18-21).

4. Some suffering may be attributed directly to the work of Satan (Job 2:7; Luke 13:16; 2 Corinthians 12:7).

5. Some suffering may be understood as God's corrective discipline (Hebrews 12:4-11).

6. Much suffering simply cannot be explained in a simplistic manner; our response must be to trust God's wisdom (Job 42:1-16).

---

that we may follow all the words of this law." God hasn't told us everything; our job is to follow faithfully in what we do know.

On this side of Heaven, there always will be some mystery to the problem of suffering. In the years shortly before Christ came, two groups of Jewish scholars, one led by Shammai and another led by Hillel, debated the question, "Might it have been better if God had never created mankind at all?" After two and one-half years of discussion, everyone finally agreed that, though it might have been better for us not to exist, we do exist, so we should consider carefully how we act!

If you find a worn, tarnished coin on the sidewalk, you may not be able to explain exactly why the coin is so dented and worn. But even in its damaged condition the coin still has value. You can still take it to a store and buy something with it. Likewise, we may not be able to explain all the reasons for our hardships here on earth. But even a tarnished, dented life has value in the eyes of God.

In the final analysis, God doesn't have to answer to anyone about why he made the world the way he did. Philip Yancey wrote a fascinating book titled, *Where Is God When It Hurts?* In it he says our "arms are too short to box with God."[4] Like Job, after asking our questions, we must simply bow before the creator and admit there are things too wonderful for us to know (see Job 42:3).

If we can't figure out everything there is to know about suffering, there are still some important things we can do. Peter says, "So then, those who suffer according to God's will should commit themselves to their faithful Creator and continue to do good" (v. 19). No matter what, we can still be committed to God. We can continue to do good. We can still put our hope in God as we look forward to an eternal dwelling place where there will be no more "death or mourning or crying or pain" (Revelation 21:4). The Bible may not tell us everything we'd like to know about the "genesis," or origin, of suffering, but it assures us there will indeed by an "exodus"—a way out.[5]

There's no "ouchless" answer to the problem of suffering. Pain is real, but so is God's concern. No matter how well we understand the problem intellectually, we struggle to deal with it emotionally when we, or others we love, writhe in pain.

A satisfying answer to the problem of evil can be found only in Jesus. He shows us that God indeed is good, for Christ lived on this planet in perfect innocence. And Jesus shows us that God indeed is all-powerful—even able to overcome death.

We could diagram it like this:

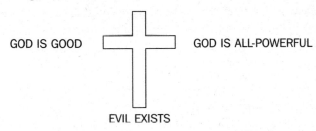

GOD IS GOOD — [cross] — GOD IS ALL-POWERFUL

EVIL EXISTS
(but ultimately has been overcome through Christ)

The cross holds the answer to the problem of evil. When all has been said and done, the answer isn't in how we handle suffering, but in how God himself handled it. He can comfort us in our sorrows because he views us much the same way he beheld his own Son on the cross—through tear-filled eyes.

NOTES: CHAPTER SEVEN

1. H. L. Mencken, in *The Critical Man*, A. M. Tibbetts, and Charlene Tibbetts, eds. (Glenview, IL: Scott, Foresman and Company, 1972), pp. 266-267.

2. Norman Geisler and Ronald M. Brooks, *When Skeptics Ask* (Wheaton, IL: Victor Books, 1990), p. 63.

3. Geisler, *Philosophy of Religion* (Grand Rapids: Zondervan, 1974), p. 329.

4. Philip Yancey, *Where Is God When It Hurts?* (Grand Rapids: Zondervan, 1977), p. 81.

5. Clark H. Pinnock, *Reason Enough* (Downers Grove, IL: InterVarsity, 1980), p. 115.

CHAPTER EIGHT

Leading From Your Knees

1 Peter 5:1-15; John 13:1-17

C an you imagine the following scenes?

You walk up to the counter at your local McDonald's, and the man who takes your order is the Chairman of the Board of the McDonald's Corporation.

You take your Chevrolet to the garage to get the brakes repaired, and the mechanic who fixes your car is none other than the Chairman of General Motors.

While on vacation in England, you arrive at London's Heathrow Airport, where Prince Charles carries your bags to a waiting taxi driven by the queen herself.

During a visit to Washington, DC, you drop your dirty laundry off at the White House so the President and First Lady can wash and press your clothes.

Wait a minute. These examples are so unrealistic, they are laughable. It's ridiculous to think that a famous, powerful, highly-ranked person would stoop down to the level of an ordinary worker. We can hardly even imagine that someone as important as a CEO, a president, or a queen would perform some humble act of service for ordinary people like us.

Yet that's exactly what happened on a spring evening in an upper room in Jerusalem. In a moment of great simplicity and high drama, the king of kings and Lord of lords—the Son of God himself— wrapped a towel around his waist, stooped down to the floor, and one by one, he washed the dust from his disciples' feet. We rightly call

Jesus the master teacher, the great physician, the wonderful counselor, but he is also the humble servant. He is the good shepherd, but he also knows how it feels to be a sheep.

Do you picture a leader as one who towers above all the rest? Jesus shows that sometimes a true leader must lead from his knees—from the position of humility and servitude.

A HUMBLING LESSON FOR PETER

This was a difficult lesson for Peter to learn. During the last supper, when Jesus began to wash his disciples' feet, Peter objected. "No," said Peter "you shall never wash my feet" (John 13:8). Isn't that just like Peter to put his foot in his mouth, when he should have been putting his best foot forward? But I can understand why Peter felt this way. Foot-washing was the work of slaves. Israel was a land of dirt roads and sandaled feet. It was a common gesture of hospitality for the host to provide a basin of water for dinner guests, and in wealthier homes it was customary for a servant to meet the guest at the door and wash his feet.

This was dirty work—the kind of job few would volunteer to do. You probably have jobs like that around your house—like cleaning the bathroom or taking out the trash.

If you're like me, you probably find it tempting to avoid tasks like those. But Jesus volunteered to do what his disciples evidently were too proud to do for one another.

No wonder Peter objected. Perhaps he remembered the time a sinful woman wept until her tears rained down on Jesus' feet; she wiped his feet with her hair, kissed his feet, and poured perfume on them (Luke 7:36-38). No doubt Peter recalled how, just a few days before the last supper, Mary (the sister of Martha and Lazarus) poured perfume on Jesus' feet and wiped his feet with her hair (John 12:1-3). Peter may have been thinking, "That's what should be happening right now. We should be washing the Lord's feet, not the other way around."

Although Peter's reluctance was understandable, a closer look shows that it was actually a shallow, pseudo humility that caused Peter to resist Jesus' foot-washing.

Peter was humble enough to recognize that he didn't deserve to have Jesus serve him, but at the same time he was proud enough to presume to tell his master what to do! Jesus offered cleansing, but Peter said in effect, "No, Lord, I'll wash my own feet, thank you." Wasn't this really just a subtle form of pride masquerading as humility?

Jesus' response was immediate and firm: "Unless I wash you, you have no part with me" (John 13:8). And this time, Peter submitted. "Then Lord," he replied, "not just my feet but my hands and head as well!" In other words, "If you insist on washing me, Lord, then wash me all over! Let me have all the cleansing I can get. Rid me of any impurity, any uncleanness, any dirt—anything at all that hinders my fellowship with you."

When Jesus finished washing his disciples' feet that night, he asked them, "Do you understand what I have done for you?" It's a good question for us to ponder too. Do we really understand servanthood? Do we really comprehend what it means to lead others from our knees?

Continuing, Jesus said, "You call me 'Teacher' and 'Lord,' and rightly so, for that is what I am. Now that I, your Lord and Teacher, have washed your feet, you also should wash one another's feet. I have set you an example that you should do as I have done for you" (John 13:12-15). Jesus gave his followers what some have termed "the new Golden Rule." No longer is the goal simply to try to "do unto others as you would have them do unto you." We have a second, more grace-oriented Golden Rule to follow: "Do unto others as *Jesus* has done unto you." Jesus went the second mile. He calls us to have a "service mentality," not a "serve us mentality."

If Jesus walked into your room tonight, would you be willing to wash his feet? Of course! But first he insists on washing yours. And then he tells you to wash the feet of your neighbors. Ironically, when you wash your neighbors' feet, in a way you're washing Jesus' feet after all. "Whatever you did for one of the least of these brothers of mine, you did for me" (Matthew 25:40).

IMPORTANT REMINDERS FOR LEADERS

First Peter was written to encourage struggling Christians whose faith was under fire. Then and now, church leaders play a vital role in determining what a congregation's attitude will be during tough times. Faithful leaders can inspire confidence and courage. On the other hand, power-hungry, pessimistic, or uncommitted leaders can drag the whole congregation down. If indeed "it is time for judgment to begin with the family of God" (1 Peter 4:12), then the leaders ought to be the first to examine themselves.

So Peter says, "To the elders among you, I appeal as a fellow elder, a witness of Christ's sufferings and one who also will share in the glory to be revealed: Be shepherds of God's flock that is under your care, serving as overseers—not because you must, but because you are willing, as God wants you to be; not greedy for money, but eager to serve; not lording it over those entrusted to you, but being examples to the flock. And when the Chief Shepherd appears, you will receive the crown of glory that will never fade away" (1 Peter 5:1-4).

Let's consider four important lessons we can discover in this text.

1. Notice *to whom Peter addresses this section of his letter*—church leaders known variously as "elders," "shepherds," and "overseers." (It's interesting that the same three words are used to describe the Ephesian elders mentioned in Acts 20:17, 28.) The word "elder" (Greek *presbyteros*) points to their age, respectability, and maturity in faith. "Shepherd" (Greek *poimen*) speaks of their pastoral function of feeding, nurturing, and protecting God's people. "Overseer" (Greek *episkopos*) refers to their personal involvement in watching over the affairs of the church. (The emphasis in this word is not on occupying a supervisory *position*, but on performing a *care-giving function*.)

In the New Testament church, a plurality of elders worked together to lead God's people. Church leadership was never meant to be a "one-man show." It takes humility to share responsibility with others and work together as a team.

2. Notice *the humble, encouraging way that Peter addresses them*. Even though he speaks with the authority of an apostle, Peter identifies him-

self with the elders by appealing to them "as a fellow elder." It's seldom easy to be a leader; church leadership is especially difficult when God's people are suffering persecution. The elders themselves may well have been suffering. They may have been the focal point of the slanderous accusations that unbelievers were spreading about the Christians. Peter knows how they feel. By calling himself a fellow elder, he's saying, "I'm with you guys. I understand what you're going through."

Peter also calls himself "a witness of Christ's sufferings and one who also will share in the glory to be revealed." He reminds the elders that he himself saw firsthand what Jesus went through on the cross, yet because Jesus also rose from the dead, there still are glorious good times ahead for God's people.

Leaders shoulder heavy responsibilities and endure a lot of criticism. When is the last time you called one of your church's leaders just to say, "Thanks for all you do"? When is the last time you sent your leaders a card or letter of encouragement? What does your congregation do to obey the Scripture's command to hold your leaders "in the highest regard in love because of their work" (1 Thessalonians 5:13)? In your church, do people try to make your leaders' work "a joy, not a burden" (Hebrews 13:17)? Or is there so much fussing, fuming, sniping, griping, nail-biting, nit-picking, foot-dragging, growth-stifling faithlessness that the leaders are nearly burned out and feel like giving up?

What could you do to appreciate and encourage your leaders more effectively?

3. Notice *what should motivate a leader.* In this section, Peter mentions three wrong motivations to avoid, and three right motivations to adopt:

• *Lead, not because you must, but willingly.* Just as God loves a cheerful giver, he also loves a cheerful elder. If you have to twist someone's arm to persuade him to be an elder, chances are he's not ready for the job. One of the qualities of a true leader is that he desires the work (see 1 Timothy 3:1) and does it willingly, not merely out of obligation.

• *Lead, not because of greed, but with eagerness to serve.* Church leaders have a right to be compensated so that their financial needs are provided and they can devote themselves fully to the work of the ministry (see 1 Corinthians 9:7-12; Galatians 6:6). This may be what Paul meant when he referred to "double-honored elders" who worked hard at their preaching and teaching (1 Timothy 5:17, 18). But a leader should never choose, or continue in, a ministry solely because of his own personal gain. People greedy for money or prestige have harmed many a church.

• *Lead, not through the power of your position, but through the influence of your example.* Leaders shouldn't "lord it over" the people entrusted to their care, but set such a compelling example that others will naturally desire to "consider the outcome of their way of life and imitate their faith" (Hebrews 13:7).

To many of us today, a "sergeant" brings to mind an authoritarian leader who bosses people around, barks orders, and makes sure his troops all march in step with his instructions. Curiously, the term is derived from the Latin *servire,* to serve. Originally, a "sergeant" was a "servant," one who served his country and his followers.

When I was working full-time as a college professor, I received in the mail an advertisement for a magazine for academic professionals. The letter used an interesting advertising pitch. It started out by telling the "horror story" of how some faculty members found themselves in a terrible position: due to cost-cutting measures at the university, they now had to vacuum the floors of their own offices and carry out their own trash. Then the letter went on to tell how subscribing to the publisher's magazine would help faculty members to avoid humiliating "mistreatment" like serving as their own janitor.

Now, don't get me wrong. I have great respect for the work of college professors. But I was struck by the blatantly condescending view this letter portrayed toward people who do manual labor and tasks like cleaning up a floor or taking out the trash. A bit of humble cleanup work never hurt anyone—even a faculty member.

For fifty years, Bernie Stowe was the equipment manager for the Cincinnati Reds baseball team. He always worked in the background, but over the years he became a fixture in the Reds organization. When Stowe finally retired after five decades of service, Hall of Fame catcher Johnny Bench pointed out, "Bernie never wore a uniform. But he washed the uniforms of almost every Red who ever played the game!"

That's not a bad tribute. Come to think of it, I've known church members who remind me of Bernie Stowe. They don't receive any cheers from the crowd, but they "wash dirty uniforms." They never stand behind the pulpit and preach, but they pray for those who do. They don't lead baptism services, but they make sure the water in the baptistery is clean and warm, and later they wash the robes and towels. They don't have their names printed in the Sunday bulletin, but they are the ones who hand a bulletin to a visitor along with a friendly handshake. They don't sing solos, take the lead in the Christmas musical, or write Christian books, but they have songs in their hearts as they serve Christ behind the scenes.

Sure, church leadership takes more than background acts of service . . . but it never takes less. Effective models of servant-leadership are desperately needed in the church today.

God is looking for people who will lead from their knees. He's searching for people of prayer and humility who will motivate others through the power of their personal example, not by handing down executive decisions from the safety of a board meeting room.

4. Notice what Peter says about *the rewards of leadership.* Lest we mistakenly conclude that leadership is an impossible task too tough to undertake, Peter offers a strong word of encouragement: "And when the Chief Shepherd appears, you will receive the crown of glory that will never fade away" (v. 4).

In an article in *Leadership,* Ed Dobson wrote about what he calls "four myths of ministry":

• It is never as bad as you think it is. Even when things seem darkest, circumstances are usually not as hopeless or as awful as they first appear.

• It's never as good as you think it is. There are times in church ministry when everything seems to be going marvelously. That's when you need to be careful.

• It's never completely fixed. Ministry is a process; it's people. To say, 'I've taken care of this problem; it won't recur' is foolish.

- It's never completely broken. . . . No matter what it looks like, God's work has not stopped.[1]

Church leadership may be tough, but it's incredibly worthwhile. There's the privilege of sharing in the work of the "chief shepherd." This translates the Greek word *archipoimenos*. It's the only New Testament term that could possibly mean something like "archbishop," and it's used only in reference to Jesus, not to men! Christ is the "pastor in chief," the overseer of the overseers, the master of the ministers.

It seems odd to me that Christian theological seminaries offer a degree for ministers called "Master of Divinity." I don't mean to sit in judgment of those who have earned this demanding degree. (It requires ninety hours of often grueling graduate study. I know; I acquired one myself.) It's just the wording that bothers me. Who could ever claim to have "mastered divinity"? No human being on earth has ever fully mastered the study of God.

It is enough just to serve our master—to learn of him and work for him with humble faith. When a church leader begins to feel discouraged and unappreciated, it's good to remember the privileges he has simply to serve the king of kings. No fancy titles, no plaques on the wall are needed. It's a high honor simply to share in the work of the chief shepherd.

In the future, there's also "the crown of glory that will never fade away." When Jesus returns to earth and shares his glorious riches with his faithful servants, the hardships of this life will seem insignificant.[1]

IMPORTANT REMINDERS FOR FOLLOWERS

A leader can't lead unless there's someone to follow. After dealing with leadership in 1 Peter 5:1-4, Peter turns to "followership." The principles here apply to all Christians, but Peter has some special words for young men: "Be submissive to those who are older" (v. 5).

PROTECT RESPECT

Respect someone simply because he's older? This may sound like a strange idea today, especially in our more youth-oriented Western culture. In Asia and the Middle East, however, deep respect for the older generation is a time-honored tradition.

One day my daughter Mindy asked me matter-of-factly, "Dad, when you were a boy, did you dress like the Pilgrims?" I assured her that I wasn't quite *that* old, but her question did make me ponder the way we view aging. Some of the most beautiful people I know are senior adults: seasoned elders who lead the church with wisdom, a kind widow who grows vegetables to share with her neighbors, the retired couple across the street who keep their lawn so carefully trimmed, a couple in their sixties who faithfully support a local church's campus ministry. Author Joseph Campbell said, "As a candle in a holy place, so is the beauty of an aged face."

Why does Peter single out the young *men* and tell them to be submissive? Shouldn't young women respect older folk too? For that matter, isn't everyone supposed to be submissive (1 Peter 2:13)? Perhaps in the specific churches Peter was addressing, there were prideful young men who needed correction. I can't speak for the ladies, but as someone who once was a young man, I can agree that humility isn't always a young guy's strong suit! One of the special temptations of youth is to be cocky and assume we know the *right* way to do things.

Soon after I became editor of THE LOOKOUT magazine, one of our regular columnists paid me a visit. Orrin Root, ninety-one years old at the time, has been involved in journalism and editorial work longer than I have been alive. For years Mr. Root has been a highly respected fixture in our company's branch of the Christian publishing business. After some good-natured teasing about what it's like to be an editor, Mr. Root told me, "Sometimes an older person gets to the point where he or she doesn't really have it anymore." I listened, unsure where he was headed with this.

"I enjoy writing my weekly column," Mr. Root continued, "but I want you to promise that you'll tell me if the quality of my work ever goes down."

I assured Mr. Root that I consider his work of the highest quality, and I promised to treat him the way I'd want someone to treat me when I am ninety-one myself.

After a bit more discussion, we laughed together and shook hands. As Mr. Root left, I shook my head in amazement and commented to one of my coworkers, "There goes one very classy guy!" How humbling it was for me, an inexperienced editor, to receive such gracious treatment from such a great man of faith.

Peter seems to be describing people like Mr. Root when he writes, "Clothe yourselves with humility toward one another, because, 'God opposes the proud but gives grace to the humble'" (1 Peter 5:5; see also Proverbs 3:34). The phrase, "clothe [gird] yourselves," reminds us again of the way Jesus clothed himself with a towel and taught his disciples about humility by washing their feet.

LEARN THE BLESSINGS OF HUMILITY

Sinful pride leads to disaster, but genuine humility enables us to experience God's fullest blessings.

Humble people are more secure. We should humble ourselves "under God's mighty hand," Peter says— like a child clinging to the hand of a loving parent, or a patient submitting to the steady hand of a surgeon. The Lord's hand is a safe place—a place of security and protection (see John 10:27-30). When we humbly trust him, God promises to lift us up "in due time" (v. 6)—not necessarily the time *we* might choose, but when the Lord knows it's right.

Humble people pray more effectively. "Cast all your anxiety on him because he cares for you" (v. 7; literally, "because to him it matters concerning you.") Why do we so often cling to our worries instead of casting them on God? Sometimes our pride gets in the way. We try to solve our problems ourselves instead of seeking the Lord's help. The word for "cast" in this verse (Greek *epiripto*) is the same word used in Luke 19:35 to describe the way the disciples threw, or cast, their garments onto the colt Jesus rode into Jerusalem at the triumphal entry. God invites us to toss our cares onto his back instead of carrying them on our own. "Praise be to the Lord, to God our Savior, who daily bears our burdens" (Psalm 68:19).

Humble people are better equipped to resist the devil. Satan is our enemy, a roaring lion "looking for someone to devour" (1 Peter 5:8). But we can "resist him, standing firm in the faith" (v. 9). The Greek word translated "resist" is *anthistemi,* a compound of two words that mean "against" and "to stand." This is where we get our "antihistamines," those helpful medicines that enable us to stand against pollen or other pollutants that irritate our allergies. If we resist the devil by leaning on God's power, the lion-like devil will prove to be a cowardly lion; he will flee from us (James 4:7).

Humble people will win out in the long run. "And the God of all grace, who called you to his eternal glory in Christ, after you have suffered a little while, will himself restore you and make you strong, firm and steadfast" (v. 10). "Blessed are the meek, for they will inherit the earth" (Matthew 5:5).

Speaker and writer Stuart Briscoe tells about a time when, as a young boy, he heard Dr. Donald Grey Barnhouse preach at a convention in England. Dr. Barnhouse began his sermon by surveying the crowd and then saying, "The way to up is down." Briscoe says, "There was a kind of rustle among the British crowd—that's hardly the way to begin a sermon." When the slight rustle ended, the preacher repeated: "The way to up is down." By then, Briscoe says, he concluded that this American preacher was "a nut," and "I switched him off and I'm sorry. Because, if as a kid I could have learned that, I might have saved myself and others a lot of trouble."[3]

What does it mean to say, "The way to up is down"? Just look at Jesus, Briscoe says. "The way to the throne was through the tomb. The way to the crown is through the cross. The way to Christ's exaltation, and the exaltation of millions of lost souls, was through the agony of Calvary. The way to a life lived in the power of God down here on earth is through humility and bowing the knee to Christ as Lord."[4]

Great leaders don't always tower above us. Often, they lead from their knees.

NOTES: CHAPTER EIGHT

1. Ed Dobson, "Renewing Your Sense of Purpose," *Leadership* (Summer, 1995), pp. 105, 106.

2. For a fuller explanation of the implications of grace-centered servant leadership, see my earlier book, *Growing Churches, Growing Leaders* (Joplin: College Press, 1994).

3. Stuart Briscoe, *Bound for Joy* (Glendale, CA: Regal Books, 1975), p. 73.

4. Ibid.

CHAPTER NINE

For Maturing Audiences Only

2 Peter 1:1-11

In his book *Seriously, Life Is a Laughing Matter*, humorist Tom Mullen pokes a bit of fun at what he calls the "hard-boiled middle-aged macho man" who looks silly when he tries to act tough. The truth, Mullen says, is that few guys over forty "deliberately perform acts of physical courage, unless we can be finished with them and in bed by 10:30 P.M. Most of us this age," he continues, "are more concerned with how *far* a car will go than how fast. Whatever aggressiveness is left is used keeping a child in college and ourselves out of debt."[1]

Mullen goes on to make some serious points about what it really means to be mature. Jesus calls us to receive the kingdom as little children. But we adults, Mullen suggests, often shrug off our children's questions with the words, "You're too young to understand, honey," while the truth is, we adults are the ones who don't understand. "Maturity means to grow up," Mullen says, "but Jesus' point is that 'growing up' should have a childlike perspective."[2]

Do we really understand what it means to be mature? Remember when there used to be a movie rating called "M"—for "mature audiences" only? It's sad, but nowadays, "mature" entertainment usually means a program that includes explicit sex scenes and vulgar language. "Adult" beverages are ones laced with alcohol, too much of which can make people act far less than mature. Isn't it strange how we tend to associate adulthood with deeper sin rather than greater righteousness—as if "adults" were somehow allowed to commit "adultery," and "maturity" could be equated with freedom to engage in "immorality"?

We need to rethink what it means to be mature. When Jesus said, "Be perfect, therefore, as your heavenly Father is perfect" (Matthew 5:48), the word translated "perfect" (Greek *teleios*) has to do with completeness, purposefulness, or maturity. As we follow Christ, he presents us with a noble, challenging goal: to be complete, to fulfill God's purpose, to reflect his holy character more fully, to join with other believers "until we all reach unity in the faith and in the knowledge of the Son of God and become mature, attaining to the whole measure of the fullness of Christ" (Ephesians 4:13). Like an owner's manual written by a manufacturer, the Bible contains our creator's guidelines for growth in maturity. As Peter grew old and saw his own death approaching, he was increasingly concerned that his fellow Christians should remain strong and press on toward maturity in their faith.

The letter we call 2 Peter is Peter's follow-up epistle to his earlier readers, intended to encourage them toward wholesome, mature thinking (see 2 Peter 1:1; 3:1). In a sense, this second book could also be viewed as Peter's "last will and testament," for these are his parting reminders written a short time before he died.[3]

The theme of 2 Peter could be summarized in the simple phrase, "Know more, and grow more." The Greek word for "knowledge" was used sixteen times in this short letter. Peter was concerned that his readers know the truth, so they could withstand the distortions of false teachers. The emphasis on *knowing* is combined with an emphasis on *growing*, at both the beginning and at the end of the book (2 Peter 1:5-11; 3:18).

Let's take a look at the opening verses of this epistle to discover what it means to mature and grow in Christ.

THE POWER TO BECOME MATURE

"His divine power has given us everything we need for life and godliness through our knowledge of him who called us by his own glory and goodness" (v. 3). God's divine power gives us the strength to become mature. He provides everything we need for life and godliness.

POWER FOR LIFE

In the summer of 1996, scientists made headlines by announcing the discovery of a meteorite, found in an ice field in Antarctica. According to some, the 4.2-pound rock allegedly from Mars appears to contain microscopic fossilized remains of bacteria-like objects. *Time* magazine (August 19, 1996) ran a feature story with the dramatic headline, "Life on Mars." The late astronomer Carl Sagan enthusiastically welcomed the news and exclaimed, "If the results are verified, it is a turning point in human history."

I can understand why scientists are interested in the Mars rock. But I'm amazed how quickly—almost desperately—folk who deny the reality of God will grasp eagerly for even the faintest indication that life arose from purely natural causes. Doesn't it make more sense to believe that the living God is the author of life, with all its form and complexity? More than a visit to our planet by a wandering meteorite from Mars, isn't history's true turning point the time when the Word became flesh and dwelt among us? Our creator's personal visit to earth is far more than an intellectual curiosity. He gives us everything we need for life.

When is the last time you thanked God simply for his gift of life? We thank him in the maternity ward when a new baby is born; do we remember to thank him when the baby has grown into a sometimes-tough-to-be-around adolescent? We thank God for life when we narrowly escape harm during a close call on the highway; do we remember to thank him for all the other moments he protects our lives and keeps us safe? We thank God for life when a loved one comes safely through hazardous surgery, but do we remember to thank him for all those days when we're blessed with good health?

It's fitting to call him the "living God." God is the author of physical life—he "made Heaven and earth and sea and everything in them" (Acts 14:15). He is also the author of spiritual life— "because of his great love for us, God, who is rich in mercy, made us alive with Christ even when we were dead in transgressions—it is by grace you have been saved" (Ephesians 2:4, 5). And God is the giver of eternal life— "For the wages of sin is death, but the gift of God is eternal life in Christ Jesus our Lord" (Romans 6:23).

POWER FOR GODLINESS

God has given us "very great and precious promises"—and he never breaks a promise (see Joshua 21:45; 1 Kings 8:56). These promises are given for a reason: "so that through them you may participate in the divine nature and escape the corruption in the world caused by evil desires" (2 Peter 1:4).

What does it mean to "participate in the divine nature"? In recent years, Shirley MacLaine and others have popularized the New Age concept that we human beings are gods ourselves. It would be a gross misunderstanding of Peter's words to think he means we are somehow absorbed into such a oneness with God that we ourselves actually become God. It's true that we participate in the divine nature. But we do this, *not* in the New Age sense, but in the *New Testament* sense!

The word translated "participate" ("partakers" in the *King James Version*) is from the Greek *koinonia,* which means "fellowship," or a sharing of something in common. Believers share wonderful fellowship with God, an intimate bond of personal relationship where his Spirit dwells in us (Acts 2:38; Romans 8:9). We never "become God," but the Holy Spirit gives us power to become more godly, more holy, and less like the sinful world around us.

THE PROCESS OF BECOMING MATURE

What do you want to accomplish in your life as you grow older? How will you find fulfillment and satisfaction with the passing of time? In his book, *Can Man Live Without God?* teacher and Christian apologist Ravi Zacharias suggests that a meaningful life includes four basic ingredients—wonder, truth, love, and security—and Christ alone fulfills all four of these needs.[4]

The book of Ecclesiastes is right. Without God, life is meaningless, a chasing after the wind. As someone has said, the greatest "disease" of our time is "dis-ease," a lack of ease, serenity, and peace. But in Christ, God offers us everything we need for life and godliness. We aren't doomed to a futile existence where we simply "live in constant suspense, filled with dread both night and day" (Deuteronomy 28:66). Our lives are filled with purpose as we apply all diligence to the worthwhile goal of becoming more mature, more Christlike, and more useful to our Savior.

DILIGENCE

Maturity isn't something we just drift into: it requires diligent effort. "For this very reason," Peter says, "make every effort to add to your faith" (v. 5).

I enjoy gardening, but when I moved into my house several years ago, the only spot for a garden was an area in my backyard where the soil was nothing but Southern Ohio clay. It took a while, but gradually I removed the rocks and weeds, dug out the hardened clay, and added compost, topsoil, sand, and fertilizer. Now my garden, small as it is, yields an annual bounty of beans, tomatoes, cucumbers, and onions.

Ultimately, only God can make things grow. But we are responsible to cooperate diligently with the laws of growth established by God. If we want to mature spiritually, there is no substitute for the basic disciplines. We need to pray, stay involved in individual and group Bible study and corporate worship, exercise our spiritual gifts, and share our faith consistently and energetically with others.

We must remember, though, to grow gracefully, depending on the strength God provides. Sometimes spiritual growth is a bit like falling asleep—the harder you try to do it, the harder it becomes.[5] By itself, human effort is inadequate, but in another sense it is indispensable. God works in us to fulfill his purpose, but we must be willing to cooperate (see Philippians 2:12, 13).

DEVELOPMENT

In 2 Peter 1:5-7, Peter lists eight qualities of the mature Christian life. These virtues are presented in a literary form known as "sorites." Each item in the list is mentioned once, then repeated before another item is added (A . . . B . . . B . . . C . . . C . . . D . . . and so on). Similar forms of expression appear in Romans 8:29, 30; 10:14, 15; James 1:15.

These virtues (faith, goodness, knowledge, self-control, perseverance, godliness, brotherly kindness, and love) are similar to the fruit of the Spirit listed in Galatians 5:22, 23. Bible commentator Michael Green refers to Peter's list as "the ladder of faith," a pattern for step-by-step progress toward spiritual maturity.[6]

I've heard of Christians who have adopted a systematic way to mature in each of these qualities. They prayerfully ask God to increase their faith each day, then try to focus on developing one of the other seven qualities every day of the week. (For example, Monday is their day to meditate on developing "goodness," Tuesday, "knowledge," and so on.) I admire these folk's motivation and self-discipline. I'm not sure, though, that spiritual maturity can always be so neatly organized and systematized. Such an approach almost sounds like trying to bake a cake by putting the flour in the mixing bowl on Monday, adding the milk on Tuesday and the eggs on Wednesday, and finally baking the cake on Thursday. You can have all the right ingredients, but still have a mess!

It seems to me that Peter's intent is mainly just to show us the kinds of qualities that are characteristic of Christian maturity as a whole. As we become more Christlike, our lives will bear these kinds of good fruit with the passing of time. It starts with the right attitude. When someone asked the great Olympic athlete Bob Mathias how he managed to leap so high in pole-vaulting and high-jumping events, he responded, "It's simple, really. First you throw your heart over the bar, and then the rest will follow."

THE RESULTS OF BECOMING MATURE

The goal of every Christian's heart should be to "possess these qualities in increasing measure" (v. 8), always pushing toward maturity. Peter warns about what will happen to people who don't grow in maturity, and he offers encouraging words about the positive results for those who do become more mature.

IF YOU DON'T GROW

Lack of growth, Peter implies, makes you "ineffective and unproductive in your knowledge of our Lord Jesus Christ" (v. 8).

Furthermore, a person who does not grow in maturity shows that "he is nearsighted and blind" (v. 9). As a nearsighted person myself, I understand quite well that nearsighted people see only what is close to them. Likewise, non-growing Christians are in danger of falling into the grip of selfishness—able to see only what directly affects their own lives. The Greek word translated "nearsighted" is *myopazein,* from which we derive our term for nearsightedness, "myopia."

Spiritual myopia is a common disorder. Sometimes whole churches seem to have a vision problem. Congregations with this affliction seldom see through eyes of faith. They try to justify their apathy and nongrowth by complaining, "Our needs aren't being met." Or, "We can't afford to send money to missionaries overseas; we need to keep our funds here at home." Or, "We don't need to set goals; we're doing well just to keep our doors open on Sunday." Or, "We don't need to grow anymore; we're already so big we don't know everyone anymore."

Worst of all, the non-growing Christian "has forgotten that he has been cleansed from his past sins" (v. 9). David wrote, "Praise the Lord, O my soul, and forget not all his benefits" (Psalm 103:2). Surely this is one of the reasons Christ told his followers to remember him by observing the Lord's Supper. We need regular reminders so we will "forget not all his benefits"—especially the way God forgave our sins through the sacrifice of Christ.

IF YOU DO GROW

There's positive news, too. For those who press on toward maturity, the picture is encouraging indeed. Maturing Christians are *more sure about our calling.* Peter says, "Therefore, my brothers, be all the more eager to make your calling and election sure" (v. 10). As we grow in God's grace we can become more confident and assured about our salvation—more appreciative of God's promise that we have eternal life (see 1 John 5:13).

Maturing Christians also are *more resistant to falling.* "For if you do these things," Peter writes, "you will never fall" (v. 10). While we all stumble in many ways (see James 3:2), there's a big difference between a temporary loss of footing and a complete and permanent fall. Sometimes maturity grows the most during hard times when our faith is under fire.

According to Peter, it will be worth it all in the long run. Those who persevere "will receive a rich welcome into the eternal kingdom of our Lord and Savior Jesus Christ" (v. 11).

A rich welcome? That's what a new baby receives from his parents. It's what a soldier receives from his family when he comes home from the battlefield. A rich welcome is what a championship team receives in its hometown after winning the World Series or the Super Bowl. It's what happens when a grandparent arrives for the Christmas holidays to delighted squeals from the grandchildren. But even more, a rich welcome is what the prodigal son received from his father upon his return home. And it's the kind of glorious homecoming the apostle Paul looked forward to after he had "fought the good fight, . . . finished the race, kept the faith" (2 Timothy 4:6-8). It's the kind of rich welcome Jesus described with the warm words, "Well done, good and faithful servant! . . . Come and share your master's happiness!" (Matthew 25:21).

Don't get discouraged when you run into some bumps on the road to maturity. A rich welcome awaits you when you come to the journey's end.

NOTES: CHAPTER NINE

1. Tom Mullen, *Seriously, Life Is a Laughing Matter* (Waco, Texas: Word, 1978), p. 50.

2. Ibid., p. 32.

3. If we view 2 Peter as Peter's "last will and testament," it can help to explain some of the stylistic differences between this letter and his earlier epistle, 1 Peter. This second letter has been described as more emotional, blunt, and "earthy" in style, as Peter uses a strong and at times unique vocabulary to express himself. In 2 Peter, the great apostle says good-bye to Christians he loves, and gives them one last exhortation to remain true to the faith in spite of the challenges of false teachers. It would be difficult to do these things without exhibiting strong emotions and using bold and expressive words.

Another possible explanation for the stylistic differences between 1 and 2 Peter is simply the suggestion that perhaps Peter used a different scribe (Silas?) to write down the first letter. In any event, it is reasonable to accept the traditional view that Peter wrote both of the epistles that bear his name. The stylistic differences between these two letters do not force us to conclude, as some have, that someone other than Peter wrote one or both of these books.

4. Ravi Zacharias, *Can Man Live Without God?* (Waco, TX: Word, 1994).

5. Mullen, *Seriously, Life Is a Laughing Matter* , p. 47.

6. Michael Green, *2 Peter and Jude* (Grand Rapids: Eerdmans, 1987), p. 75.

CHAPTER TEN

Eyewitness News

2 Peter 2:12-21

Christian faith is under fire from many directions today. For example, have you heard how the Jesus Seminar is trying to rewrite history? The approximately seventy-five liberal scholars associated with this group have gained a lot of media attention in recent years as they have questioned or openly denied the biblical view of Christ. Since the mid-1980s, this group, organized by former University of Montana biblical studies professor Robert W. Funk, has attacked the New Testament record from many angles—challenging the historical accuracy of accounts of Jesus' life, the reliability of New Testament records of Jesus' words, and the fact of Jesus' resurrection. Perhaps a more accurate title for this group might be the "*Discredit Jesus Seminar.*"

Unfortunately, this variety of skepticism is nothing new. In the 1700s, Thomas Paine—who wrote *Common Sense* and *The Age of Reason*, said, "There is no history written at the time Jesus Christ is said to have lived that speaks of the existence of such a person, even such a man."[1] The well-known skeptic Bertrand Russell wrote in his essay *Why I Am Not a Christian*, "Historically it is quite doubtful whether Christ ever existed at all, and if he did we know nothing about him."[2] In 1992, an Egyptian author named Ahmed Osman made headlines with his *The House of the Messiah*. He claimed, "There is not a shred of historical evidence that Jesus lived at the time he is supposed to have done and I believe the writers of the Gospels adapted a historical figure into their own time."[3]

While outrageous statements such as these make Christians angry, they also compel us to ask ourselves some hard questions: What evidence shows that the Bible is historically accurate? How can we respond to the charge that Jesus was not a real historical figure? Can we be sure about what Jesus said and did? How can we explain these facts to our doubtful friends and neighbors?

In 2 Peter 2:12-21, Peter offers several helpful insights that can help our faith stand up under the fire of modern criticism.

A MESSAGE TO REMEMBER

"So I will always remind you of these things, even though you know them and are firmly established in the truth you now have" (v. 12). Why did Peter think it was necessary to remind his readers of things they already knew? Repetition can be dull. Many of us would rather not eat the same kind of food or wear the same clothes day after day. Nor do we enjoy hearing a preacher or teacher say the same thing over and over.

However, sometimes repetition is not only helpful but necessary. In baseball, when a batter gets on base, the coaches need to remind him about the number of outs. When a space shuttle astronaut gets ready for blastoff, he goes through a lengthy checklist of reminders to make sure everything is safe and ready. A wedding ring serves as a healthy reminder of a married person's commitment. It may be annoying, but a warning bell inside a car can save a life by reminding the driver to fasten the seat belt.

Peter's readers already were familiar with the truth he was telling them, but they still needed an occasional reminder. In fact, Peter considered it a solemn duty to remind them about the facts that undergirded their faith.

Preachers and Sunday school teachers need to be creative enough to unearth interesting new facts from God's Word. But in our rush to be relevant, let's not forget the basics! Often we just need to remind our listeners and students about the "unflashy" but vital facts of the faith. The importance of such reminders is increasing, for biblical illiteracy is so widespread we can't assume that people know the basic teachings of the Bible. Nor should we make the mistake of assuming that, just because we preached or taught on a certain subject in the past, we never need to talk about it again. Even those who have been Christians a long time need to be reminded to walk close to the Lord. "Let us live up to what we have already attained" (Philippians 3:16). "Just as you received Christ Jesus as Lord, continue to live in him" (Colossians 2:6).

During my more than twenty years as a preacher, I have spent plenty of time wrestling with contemporary topics and culturally relevant issues. But I've also found myself appreciating times like Good Friday and Easter more with each passing year, for they help to remind me what being a Christian is all about. In our pursuit of relevance, let's not forget to "tell the old, old story of Jesus and his love." We must tell it in fresh, creative ways—but let's be careful not to let our creativity overshadow the message.

Peter writes, "I think it is right to refresh your memory as long as I live in the tent of this body" (2 Peter 1:13). "Refresh" or "stir up" (Greek *diegeiro*) means "to arouse or awaken." It was used to describe the way Jesus' disciples woke him as he slept through a storm on the Sea of Galilee (Mark 4:38; Luke 8:24). Peter wanted to rouse his readers from spiritual slumber (compare Revelation 3:2). He didn't want them to forget about God's saving work (see 2 Peter 1:9).

Does your memory need to be refreshed? How well do you recall the Word of God? We don't hear a lot about the discipline of Scripture memorization these days. Of course, there's no guarantee that we'll really live differently just because we have committed some Bible verses to memory. Yet the more we internalize the Word, the more we can meditate on it and let it change our thinking and attitude (see Deuteronomy 6:4-9; Psalm 1:2).

My friend Dan Burton, a missionary in Ethiopia, wrote in a letter about something that happened a few years ago in that country:

> Right before the Communists took over, a lot of the churches assigned Scripture to people in the church to memorize so that when the church doors closed—which they knew eventually was going to happen, and all were forced to officially close—they knew a lot of their Scriptures were going to be taken

away, and they wanted to have the Bibles memorized as much as they could. The people would memorize different sections so they could reproduce the Scriptures when the churches were closed and the Bibles were confiscated.

Dan concluded, "It would be interesting to see if we had that zeal today. People don't recognize what a privilege it is to have the Word of God. Maybe we would do a little more memorizing if we did."

The psalmist wrote, "I have hidden your word in my heart that I might not sin against you" (Psalm 119:11). When our faith comes under fire, we'll be glad we've internalized God's truth.

Peter writes, "I think it is right to refresh your memory as long as I live" (1:13).

Note the phrase, "as long as I live." There is encouragement here for senior adults. When he wrote his earlier letter, Peter already referred to himself as an elder (1 Peter 5:1). Now he was approaching death. But there was still important work for him to do in God's kingdom. As Bible commentator Bruce Oberst noted, "Peter did not plan to put himself 'on the shelf' in his older years."[4] We should serve the Lord to our fullest capacity as long as we live.

Notice that Peter refers to the "tent of this body." Did you ever camp out and sleep in a tent? Would you like to do that all the time? A tent isn't a permanent dwelling place. You live in it for a while, then you take it down, fold it up, and move on. To update the word picture, we could say our bodies are like hotels. When you stay in a hotel, the towels and beds and TV are not yours to keep forever. You stay in the hotel for a short time, then you go home to your permanent place of residence. "Now we know that if the earthly tent we live in is destroyed, we have a building from God, an eternal house in Heaven, not built by human hands" (2 Corinthians 5:1).

Peter considered these reminders urgent because he saw that he would "soon put aside" the tent of his body; Jesus had made clear to him that it wouldn't be long until Peter would die (v. 14). More than thirty years earlier, Jesus had predicted in veiled but ominous terms, that Peter eventually would die an abrupt, forcible death: "When you are old you will stretch out your hands, and someone else will dress you and lead you where you do not want to go" (John 21:18). (Since Jesus told Peter this would happen when he was old, perhaps this was one of the reasons Peter slept so soundly when Herod put him in prison and threatened him with death, as recorded in Acts 12. Peter wasn't worried, because the Lord had foretold that he wouldn't die until he was old. Plus, no matter when Peter might die, he was filled with "living hope," 1 Peter 1:3.)

Peter assured his readers, "I will make every effort to see that after my departure you will always be able to remember these things" (v. 15). "Departure" might seem like an unusual way of describing death, but it's quite meaningful. It's the Greek word *exodos,* literally the "way out," bringing to mind the way God led the Hebrews out of Egypt and into the promised land. The same Greek word was used in reference to Jesus' "departure," or death (Luke 9:31). Christians are "way-out people"! For many, death appears to be an inescapable trap. But we know the way out. For the Christian, death is our "exodus"—an exit, not an extinction or extermination. It's a departure, a time when we move from one realm into another. As someone has said, "Earth's *exodus* is Heaven's *genesis.*"

Christ's victory over death is so important to remember that the Lord gave us a special command to recall it. For people whose faith is under fire, the Lord's Supper provides a consistent reminder of the great truths that undergird our hope.

A MESSAGE BASED ON FACTS

"We did not follow cleverly invented stories when we told you about the power and coming of our Lord Jesus Christ, but we were eyewitnesses of his majesty" (v. 16). Notice the contrast Peter draws between what the Christian gospel *isn't* and what the gospel *is*—what we do, and what we don't do as Christians.

WE DON'T FOLLOW CLEVERLY INVENTED STORIES

When I was a little boy, I loved to crawl onto my grandfather's lap and listen to him tell stories. Grandpa had a wide range of tall tales at his disposal—many of which he no doubt made up as he went along. As he droned on about the giant fish he'd caught, the terrible winter storms he'd weathered, and the famous people he'd met, the tales grew taller with each retelling. There might have been a kernel of truth in some of the stories, I don't know. It didn't matter. The stories were entertaining, and the moments with Grandpa were priceless.

Many of today's critics suggest that the biblical accounts are much like my grandfather's stories—mere legends that have grown into firmly established religious traditions after centuries of retelling. "Oh, maybe they possess a kernel of truth," the critic reasons, "but the Bible stories have little basis in fact."

Peter wouldn't accept such arguments. He said we don't follow "cleverly invented stories." Here Peter employs the Greek word *muthois,* from which we derive our word "myths." Apparently some folk in the first century were already attacking the integrity of the gospel by suggesting that Jesus' words and deeds were merely myths or legends. The apostle Paul encountered similar arguments that threatened to undermine the faith (see 1 Timothy 1:4; 2 Timothy 4:4; Titus 1:14).

Attorney Norman Anderson wrote a book called *A Lawyer Among the Theologians* in which he argued that, from an objective point of view, it's difficult to dispute the overall accuracy and persuasiveness of the New Testament record.[5] Another attorney and former judge, Herbert C. Casteel, wrote the following in his book *Beyond a Reasonable Doubt:*

> Every important event that actually occurs is connected to other events that precede and follow it. There is a cause and effect relationship that cannot be faked. To falsely insert the story of Jesus into the history of the world is impossible. His life was lived at the crossroads of the ancient world, where the Hebrew, Greek, and Roman cultures all met, and His life had a vast and immediate effect on all three cultures. Take out the life of Jesus, and much of history becomes unexplainable.[6]

An honest look at the evidence shows how unlikely it is that the writers of Scripture were simply passing on myths and legends. If they were merely making up stories, they wouldn't have surrounded their writings with so many historical checkpoints. Consider the following:

If the Bible is nothing but myth, then why did the writers fill their books with specific historical and geographical details? Biblical authors mention kings, governors, countries, cities, mountains, rivers, and other locations with remarkable accuracy. Luke, for example, "names thirty-two countries, fifty-four cities, and nine islands without making a single error."[7]

If the Bible is nothing but myth, then why does archaeology offer so much physical evidence that the Scripture's message is true? For example, a traveler to the Holy Land today can wade through Hezekiah's tunnel (2 Kings 20:20) and the pool of Siloam (John 9:7).

If the Bible is nothing but myth, then why were the original disciples willing to die rather than stop preaching their message? The clear testimony of Scripture and history alike is that these early believers were convinced that their message was genuine and Jesus was truly risen from the dead. They weren't merely passing along an inspirational spiritual story; they were willing to lay down their lives for the sake of the undeniable life-changing truth that had gripped their souls.

If the Bible is nothing but myth, then why do even secular historians support the facts mentioned in the New Testament? For example, the first-century Jewish historian Josephus corroborates numerous details about the Herod family, John the Baptist, and the Pharisees; the first-century Roman historian Tacitus referred to the fact of Christ's death by order of Pontius Pilate. A Roman provincial governor, Pliny the Younger (A.D. 62-113) wrote about the Christians' high morals, their determined faith, and their regular meetings for worship and communal meals.

If the Bible is nothing but myth, then why do biblical authors relate even the flaws and mistakes of heroes like Moses, David, and Peter? Scripture is remarkably honest in its portrayal of even its main characters.

Peter is right. Christians don't just follow cleverly invented stories.

WE DO BELIEVE THE EYEWITNESS ACCOUNTS

"We were eyewitnesses of his majesty," Peter insists (v. 16). Eyewitness testimony has always played an important role in civil law. Under the Law of Moses, no one could be convicted of a crime or sentenced to capital punishment on the testimony of merely one witness; others had to back up the accusations (Deuteronomy 17:6; 19:15).

How strong is the eyewitness testimony about the life of Jesus Christ? His words and deeds were heard and recorded firsthand by careful observers like Matthew and John. Luke, trained as a physician, carefully investigated and documented what he wrote (Luke 1:1-4). When Peter and the other apostles testified about Jesus' resurrection on the Day of Pentecost, they stood just a short distance from the empty tomb. Thus, they could say without fear of contradiction, "God has raised this Jesus to life, and we are all witnesses of the fact" (Acts 2:32). More than five hundred people eventually saw the resurrected Christ (1 Corinthians 15:6). John said that he and the other apostles were simply reporting that "which we have heard, which we have seen with our eyes, which we have looked at and our hands have touched" (1 John 1:1).

Unbelievers sometimes charge that the New Testament witnesses were biased, since they already had committed themselves to following Jesus. Admittedly, a person's bias can color his testimony. I heard CBS News anchorman Dan Rather speak at a Chamber of Commerce luncheon. Rather said, "My job is to be an honest broker of information." Yet he went on to admit, "Bias is a problem with news coverage— including my own." He pointed out as well that those who view his telecasts filter their understanding through biases of their own.

Indeed, we must admit there's a sense in which Jesus' original disciples were biased. At first, they were biased *against* accepting the truth! Repeatedly, the Scriptures show how reluctant and unwilling Jesus' followers were to grasp the idea that he indeed must die and rise again (Matthew 16:21-23; Mark 9:9, 10; Luke 24:9-12, 24:25-27, 41; John 20:9). Even after Jesus rose from the dead, doubtful disciples like Thomas were slow to recognize the facts. Jesus' followers were not so naive and gullible they would believe just anything; they were realistic enough that they were convinced only after the Lord "showed himself to these men and gave many convincing proofs that he was alive. He appeared to them over a period of forty days and spoke about the kingdom of God" (Acts 1:3). Finally they were convinced. Shortly before ascending back to Heaven, the Lord gave his disciples one more lesson in understanding the Scriptures, and commissioned them with the words, "You are witnesses of these things" (Luke 24:44-49). The eyewitness news they carried to the world stands at the foundation of our faith.

Several times during his own encounters with Jesus, Peter at first was slow to understand and accept what was happening. For example, Peter seems to have been especially impressed the time when he witnessed Jesus' transfiguration. On the "sacred mountain" that day, Peter was an *eyewitness*—he and his companions saw Jesus' glory and Moses and Elijah with him (Luke 9:32). He was also an *earwitness*—he heard God's voice saying, "This is my Son, whom I love; with him I am well pleased" (2 Peter 1:17, 18; see also Matthew 17:5). Most of all, he was an *awed witness*—stunned by the majestic glory of Christ, mumbling his impulsive suggestion about building three shelters for Jesus, Moses, and Elijah (Mark 9:5, 6).

There are many mysteries to faith. But faith is not unreasonable; indeed, the Lord wants us to love him with our intellects, or minds (see Matthew 22:37). Our faith is undergirded by the solid historical evidence of eyewitness testimony. When your faith comes under fire, it's good to remember that the message of Scripture is based on facts, not fables.

A MESSAGE GIVEN BY GOD

Wise words are like "goads," like a collection of "firmly embedded nails—given by one Shepherd" (Ecclesiastes 12:11). This certainly is true of Scripture. Like a goad (a sharpened stick used to prod livestock), God's Word prods and motivates us to do what is right. Like firmly embedded nails, God's Word holds things together and brings a sense of firmness and stability to our lives.

A SURE WORD

When Peter says, "And we have the word of the prophets made more certain" (2 Peter 1:19), he does not mean to imply that there was something lacking in the message of the Old Testament prophets. He simply means that the prophecies were verified by what Jesus' apostles saw, heard, and recorded. Today we are blessed to live in the bright light of New Testament revelation, with even more reasons to believe than in the past.

Like a parent cautioning a child, or a teacher giving instructions to her class, Peter reminds his readers, "You will do well to pay attention" to this sure message from God. God's Word is like "a light shining in a dark place"—a lamp to our feet and a light for our path (Psalm 119:105)—given to guide Christians "until the day dawns and the morning star rises in your hearts" (v. 19).

It seems natural to understand the rising of the "morning star" as a reference to the second coming of Christ, since other Scriptures associate Jesus with the morning star (Revelation 2:28; 22:16; Numbers 24:17). Another view is that since Peter speaks about a new, brighter day rising "in our hearts," perhaps he's talking about our personal growth in maturity and Christlikeness (see Galatians 4:19; Ephesians 5:14).

AN INSPIRED WORD

"Above all, you must understand that no prophecy of Scripture came about by the prophet's own interpretation. For prophecy never had its origin in the will of man, but men spoke from God as they were carried along by the Holy Spirit" (vv. 20, 21).

The Bible didn't originate in the unenlightened imaginations of naive religionists. Writers of Scripture carefully wrote down what they observed and received from God.

While the Bible is historically accurate, it contains far more than merely the unaided observations of the human authors. Those who served as God's prophets were "carried along" by God's Spirit. (The Greek word *pheromene* was a sailing term, used in Acts 27:15-17 to describe how a ship was moved along by the wind.) God's true

prophets were willing to mentally "raise their sails" through their obedient, receptive attitude, and then, like a powerful wind, the Spirit
helped them say and write what God wanted.

How much does your Bible mean to you? In the early years of my
first preaching ministry, I wrote a little poem in my church newsletter.
Looking back, I realize how corny my poem was—filled with terrible,
awkwardly rhymed lines like "Let's get ready to go to Heaven, as we
serve in 1977." When my grandfather, who was aging and in ill health,
received my newsletter, he wrote me a gracious and encouraging
note—and his whole letter was a poem as well. I laughed as I read
words penned in Grandpa's own shaky handwriting: "Dear Grandson
and Granddaughter David and Candy, at rhyme and rhythm you're
becoming right handy . . . . So keep up what you're doing with your
usual ambition, and we'll be behind you with our usual best-wishin'!"

Now, by most literary standards, Grandpa's letter wasn't a great
piece of writing. But after more than twenty years, I still have that letter. In fact, I treasure it. How grateful I am that my loving grandparent
cared enough to write and encourage me in my ministry.

Since Grandpa died, I can't see him in person now, but I treasure the
letter he wrote me. Aren't you glad Peter and the other eyewitnesses of
Christ wrote down what they saw? Aren't you glad the Lord assisted
and guided them in the process? Aren't you thankful that the Lord preserved his life-giving Word through the centuries so you can study and
learn his will today?

As the apostle Paul put it, "All Scripture is God-breathed and is
useful for teaching, rebuking, correcting and training in righteousness"
(2 Timothy 3:16).

That's good to remember when your faith is under fire.

NOTES: CHAPTER TEN

1. Calvin Blanchard, ed., *The Complete Works of Thomas Paine* (Chicago: Belford, Clark & Company, 1885), p. 234.

2. Bertrand Russell, "Why I Am Not a Christian," in *The Basic Writings of Bertrand Russell,* Robert Egner and Lester Denonn, eds. (New York: Simon & Schuster, 1961), p. 62.

3. Graham Heathcote, "Egyptian Claims King Tut Model for Jesus Christ," *The Parkersburg News,* May 29, 1992.

4. Bruce Oberst, *I and II Peter* (Joplin: College Press, 1988), p. 277.

5. Norman Anderson, *A Lawyer Among the Theologians* (Grand Rapids: Eerdmans, 1973).

6. Herbert C. Casteel, *Beyond a Reasonable Doubt* (Joplin: College Press, 1990), p. 134.

7. Norman Geisler and Ron Brooks, *When Skeptics Ask: A Handbook on Christian Evidences* (Wheaton: Victor Books, 1989), p. 201.

Dances With Wolves

2 Peter 2:1-22

Kevin Costner's award-winning film, "Dances With Wolves" captured the attention of moviegoers a few years ago by portraying a soldier's experiences in the Old West. Wolves are not the focal point of the film, but they are presented sympathetically. The movie suggests that, like the Native Americans who are misunderstood and mistreated, the wolves are part of the natural environment and are to be preserved and respected.

Wolves get a far less positive portrayal in Scripture. A natural enemy of sheep and goats, wolves usually are described as dangerous predators—symbols of evil people who bring harm and destruction (as in Jeremiah 5:6; Ezekiel 22:27; John 10:12). Jesus warned his disciples that he was sending them forth "like lambs among wolves" (Luke 10:3). False prophets, the Lord foretold, will "come to you in sheep's clothing, but inwardly they are ferocious wolves" (Matthew 7:15). The apostle Paul cautioned the Ephesian elders that "savage wolves will come in among you and will not spare the flock" (Acts 20:29). Sharp warnings like these sound harsh in our day, when many people assume there is no real right or wrong way to believe or live—but perhaps that's the very reason such words of warning are needed today.

There are wolves with whom we should not dance!

The writers of Scripture often made their point by presenting contrasts between opposites: life and death, light and darkness, truth and falsehood, good and evil, the fruit of the Spirit rather than the works of the flesh. Second Peter 2 presents another striking contrast.

Immediately after telling how true prophecy originated with the Spirit of God (2 Peter 1:16-21), Peter turns to what may well be the very heart of this second epistle: a warning about false prophets.[1] The contrast is very sharp. God's Word is true, factual, healthy, and life-giving; the doctrines of false teachers are destructive, misleading, and deadly. To listen to these dangerous messages is to dance with wolves.

DANCING TO THE WRONG BEAT

This problem isn't new. In the past, "there were also false prophets among the people" (v. 1). The Greek word is *pseudoprophetai*—they were "pseudo prophets," pretenders, frauds. Not only did they falsely claim to be prophets, what they said was false as well. Both the character of the men and the content of their message were untrustworthy and misleading.

According to the Old Testament, back in Jeremiah's day false prophets exhibited characteristics like these:

1. They filled people with false hopes.
2. They spoke visions from their own minds.
3. They promised peace, when there was no peace.
4. They claimed to have special dreams, but the dreams were the delusions of their own minds, not revealed truth from God.
5. They wagged their own tongues, but claimed that God was speaking through them.
6. They hurt people with reckless lies. (See Jeremiah 23:16-32.)

Ezekiel warned against false prophets whose messages were like flimsy walls covered with whitewash so they would look more substantial than they really were (Ezekiel 13:1-12).

Likewise, Peter says, "There will be false teachers among you" (1 Peter 2:1). Here the Greek word is *pseudodidaskaloi,* "pseudo teachers." These folk may not claim to be prophets, but will teach an untrue message nonetheless. Peter's words echo Paul's ominous prediction: "The Spirit clearly says that in later times some will abandon the faith and follow deceiving spirits and things taught by demons" (1 Timothy 4:1).

Peter quickly notes several reasons false teachers are so dangerous.

MISLEADING METHODOLOGY

It would be helpful if false teachers were required to wear name tags like the bumper sticker I once saw on a car that read, "Don't Follow Me—I'm Lost!" But the fact is, false teachers "secretly introduce" their views (v. 1). They don't get up in church one Sunday morning and announce, "By the way, tonight at 7:30 we'll hold a special Bible study in which we plan to introduce doctrines that will deceive and enslave you. Everyone interested in our False Prophecy Fellowship Group, just sign the list on the bulletin board, and we'll see you tonight!" Like Satan himself, corrupt leaders are subtle, devious, cunning, and manipulative.

Today's cults sometimes use less-than-ethical methods to win and keep converts. In *Churches That Abuse,* Ronald M. Enroth notes that strong, control-oriented leaders in abusive churches "use guilt, fear, and intimidation to manipulate members and keep them in line."[2] In *The Subtle Power of Spiritual Abuse,* David Johnson and Jeff Van Vonderen comment:

> A mark of false spiritual leadership is people who, in their effort to look good, *lie.* They don't talk straight. They rarely say what they mean, and because of that, some of their followers may actually sense that these people are hard to trust. In conversations, everything seems somehow veiled, or hidden, or these people are told they are not spiritual enough to understand teachings or decisions of the leaders. The leaders sound pious enough, even spiritual. But we are left with the vague sense that something is missing. They will give you the 'right' answer, but rarely will you get the 'real' answer. Everything has a double meaning. One result is that you cannot confront them or pin anything down. It will be hard to know where you stand.[3]

DESTRUCTIVE HERESY

The false teachers, Peter says, will introduce "destructive heresies." Ordinarily we use the word "heresy" as a generic term for false doctrine. Originally, though, the Greek *hairesis* carried a somewhat different connotation, denoting a divisive or sectarian attitude. A "heretic" in this sense was one who chose to separate himself from others into a particular sect or group. Thus the word could describe the "*party* of the Sadducees" (Acts 5:17), or the "*party* of the Pharisees" (Acts 15:5). When people misidentified Christians as merely a subsect of Judaism, they accused Paul of being a "ringleader of the Nazarene *sect*" (Acts 24:5). Elsewhere in the New Testament, the word is used for the cliquish "differences" among the Corinthian believers (1 Corinthians 11:19), "factions" as a sinful work of the flesh (Galatians 5:20), and "contentious" behavior in a believer who divides the church (Titus 3:10).

It's important to consider that heresy is not only a matter of proclaiming erroneous doctrine; it is also a matter of having a contentious or divisive attitude. Evidently you could believe the right things, yet still be a "heretic" if you possessed a quarrelsome, divisive, sectarian attitude. In a day when church splits continue to cause immeasurable harm to the work of Christ, we need to take to heart the solemn biblical warnings against causing division (1 Corinthians 1:10-13; Jude 19).

MISTAKEN THEOLOGY

Today, Satan's lies are hawked openly by New Age bookstores and TV's Psychic Friends Network. Perhaps more dangerously, unbiblical concepts increasingly find their way into our cultural mainstream, promoted subtly by music, movies, and celebrity speakers. While "spirituality" is in today, biblical doctrine is out. Universalism—the idea that everyone will be saved regardless of what he believes or does—is widely assumed to be true. Tolerance is so widely valued that anyone who brands anything as "wrong" risks wearing the label of "bigot." The popular attitude seems to be, "It's OK to worship any god you want, just don't impose your ideas on others."

The problem is, faddish faith can lead people to "denying the sovereign Lord who bought them" (2 Peter 2:1). This short description identifies two significant doctrinal problems: *denying the sovereign Lord himself* and *denying or misinterpreting the Lord's saving work.*

Another way to say it is, false teachers propagate mistaken ideas about either the *person* or the *work* of Christ. Early in church history, groups like the Gnostics denied that Christ was the divine Son of God who came in real human flesh. In a sense, the incarnation is a mystery beyond our comprehension; nevertheless, Scripture clearly points to both the full humanity and the full divinity of Christ (John 1:1, 14, 18; Philippians 2:5-11; Colossians 2:8, 9; Hebrews 2:14; 1 John 4:1-3).

Verses like these are helpful when we encounter the teachings of groups like the Jehovah's Witnesses (who teach that Christ is a created being—"a god," but not one in nature with God the Father) or members of the Christian Science church, which clouds the biblical picture of personal redemption by teaching that salvation is mainly a matter of being saved from "wrong thinking" rather than a genuine removal of our guilt through the sacrifice of Christ on the cross.

As Peter shows, false teachings turn things around. They are the exact opposite of what we should believe. Jesus said, "I am the way and the truth and the life" (John 14:6). But those who follow false teachers adopt "their shameful ways," "bring the way of truth into disrepute," and fall into "condemnation" instead of life (2 Peter 2:2, 3).

SURPRISING POPULARITY

You'd think that no one would want to follow the kind of people Peter is describing. Yet the apostle warns, "Many will follow their shameful ways" (v. 2).

Numerical growth is a desirable goal for a church. In the New Testament it was cause for rejoicing when "more and more men and women believed in the Lord and were added to their number" (Acts 5:14). It's important to remember, though, that you can't always measure a message's validity by the number of people who adhere to it. Sometimes the crowd is wrong. Majority vote is not the final test of truth. According to Jesus, the wide gate and broad road lead to destruction (Matthew 7:13).

SHAMEFUL DISHONESTY

Corrupt church leaders "will bring the way of truth into disrepute" (2 Peter 2:2). How true! Dishonest, greedy Christians discredit the cause of Christ, cause weak believers to stumble, and give unbelievers one more reason to doubt the credibility of the gospel. When Jesus' disciples live by an ethical double standard, we're behaving like an army that gives guns and bullets to the enemy soldiers—we're simply giving more ammunition to Satan's army.

A few years ago, a series of well-publicized scandals involving television evangelists hit the front pages. These sad, highly visible personal tragedies immediately served as an opportunity for critics of the church to contend almost gleefully, "It's just as we always thought—Christians are hypocrites, and the people who preach the hardest against sin are committing the very sins they condemn!"

In 1993, when David Koresh and his Branch Davidian sect holed up in their compound near Waco, Texas, skeptical people shook their heads and sighed, "That's what happens when you get too serious about the Bible—you become a religious fanatic!"

Greedy teachers, Peter warns, "will exploit you with stories they have made up" (v. 3). "Exploit" is from a Greek word (*emporeuomai*) also used in James 4:13 with the idea of "selling" or "transacting business." It's wrong to turn God's church into nothing but a marketing opportunity where people are exploited so someone can make more money. "Stories" translates the Greek *plastos,* from which we get our word "plastic." Unethical leaders teach a plastic message; they simply mold or shape their words to fit their audience instead of boldly proclaiming God's truth.

MORE FALSE STEPS

With a flurry of picturesque descriptions similar to the kind used in Jude's epistle (see Jude 3-19), Peter continues to paint a vivid portrait of the "wolves" with whom we must not "dance."

We can use the word DANGER as an acrostic to summarize six more dangerous marks of false teachers:

Disrespect. They "despise authority" (v. 10).

Arrogance. Such people are "bold and arrogant" (v. 10) and "mouth empty, boastful words" (v. 18). The word for "boastful" is *huperogka,* which means "swelling" or something unnaturally swollen or puffed up. Arrogant people are like a balloon filled with nothing but hot air.

Nastiness. Like someone with greasy, oil-stained hands who handles a beautiful white wedding dress, these folk soil the purity of the church with obscenity. They are "blots and blemishes" (v. 13) who bring a vulgar, dirty perspective to everything they touch. They have

"eyes full of adultery" (v. 14). In other words, they can hardly look at
another person without thinking of sexual involvement. More than
merely an outward act, sexual sin begins with a person's attitude and
motivation (Matthew 5:27, 28). It's wise to imitate Job, who made "a
covenant" with his eyes that he would not look upon another person
with sinful lust (Job 31:1).

Greed. As "experts in greed," (v. 14) fake Christians like these know
how to manipulate people and situations to their own advantage. The
word "experts" translates the Greek *gumnazo,* from which we get our
word "gymnasium." It's as if such folk practice, exercise, or train themselves in the art of greed.

Emptiness. "These men are springs without water and mists driven by
a storm" (v. 17). If you're thirsty, you're delighted when you find a
spring of water that promises to quench your thirst. How frustrating it
would be to discover that the spring or well is empty and dry—as
unfulfilling and unsatisfying as a mirage in the desert. Like rain clouds
that promise refreshment but blow over without watering the parched
land, false teachers don't make good on their promises—they leave you
empty, dry, still thirsty for the truth. "Like clouds and wind without rain
is a man who boasts of gifts he does not give" (Proverbs 25:14).

Jeremiah said that false gods are nothing but broken cisterns hewn
out of rock. They crack, leak, and hold nothing but stagnant water;
but the true God is like a fresh, satisfying spring of living water
(Jeremiah 2:13; compare John 4:13, 14; 7:37, 38).

Restrictions. Ironically, people sometimes get involved with cults
because they want to be free from the restrictions of traditional faith,
only to find themselves locked into a system of authoritarian control.
One characteristic of cults is enslavement (financial, psychological, or
sexual) to a person or organization. Often there is little true liberty for
an individual to sit down with his Bible and decide for himself how he
will handle his time or money. False teachers "promise them freedom,
while they themselves are slaves of depravity—for a man is a slave to
whatever has mastered him" (v. 19). In *Churches That Abuse,* Ronald
Enroth warns: "In all totalitarian environments, dependency is necessary for subjugation."[4] In a misguided quest for spiritual freedom, cult

members often end up in bondage to sin, or in the firm control of an authoritarian leader.

James Dobson tells how certain elephants in India are trained to serve their human masters through a series of "brainwashing" techniques. The animals are isolated for three days, then brought to a nighttime ceremony of fire where, for hours, men intimidate them by screaming in the flickering light. By daybreak their wills are broken, and the elephants yield to their masters—as Dobson says, "transformed from freedom to slavery in a single evening."[5]

In confusing times of loneliness and isolation, bombarded by the powerful demands of peer pressure, many people exchange their individual walk with God for the freedom-stealing demands of religious charlatans.

LEARNING THE RIGHT STEPS

So how can we keep from "dancing with wolves"? Let me offer four suggestions based on the "dancing" metaphor.

• *Listen to the rhythms of righteousness.* As Peter points out, God "rescued Lot, a righteous man, who was distressed by the filthy lives of lawless men" (v. 7). Lot had his weak points (see Genesis 19:6-35), but at least he was sensitive enough to the will of God that the wicked things going on around him in Sodom and Gomorrah bothered him. He was vexed, upset, distraught because of the moral decline of his culture. "Living among them day after day, [Lot] was tormented in his righteous soul by the lawless deeds he saw and heard" (v. 8).

Do you ever read the newspaper or watch something on TV and find yourself feeling upset, angry, and irritated because of what's happening in the world? Good! You're listening to the rhythms of righteousness! We must never become so accustomed to profanity, violence, and immorality that we meet them with an unblinking shrug. If evil ceases to bother us, our hearts must be hard indeed.

• *Choose the right partner.* You don't have to join arms with those who will lead you away from Christ. Jesus himself refused to "dance" to the tune of demanding religious leaders (Matthew 11:16, 17). False teachers are not in partnership with the Spirit of God (Jude 19). It's only when we "keep in step with the Spirit" that we can keep ourselves from being burdened "by a yoke of slavery" (Galatians 5:1, 25).

• *Lend a hand to other "dancers."* Be ready to help others who are in danger of falling victim to the devil's schemes. The prime targets of cults are young people and new Christians who are not yet firmly rooted in their faith. False teachers "seduce the unstable" (v. 14) and "entice people who are just escaping from those who live in error" (v. 18). It's easier to harm a baby than a full-grown man; lambs are especially vulnerable to wolves. Be alert and help others avoid spiritual danger.

• *Remember what will happen when the "dance" is over.* At the end of life, those who deny Christ face condemnation and destruction (v. 3); they will perish (v. 12); "they will be paid back with harm for the harm they have done" (v. 13); "blackest darkness is reserved for them" (v. 17); "they are worse off at the end than they were at the beginning" (v. 20).

In 2 Peter 2:4-9, Peter shows that there is a divine logic at work—a "truth or consequences" choice presented to mankind. If in the past God judged angels (and he did); if God judged the wicked world of Noah's day (and he did); if God judged the evil cities of Sodom and Gomorrah (and he did); and if he rescued someone like Lot who was willing to believe (and he did); "then the Lord knows how to rescue godly men from trials and to hold the unrighteous for the day of judgment" (v. 9).

To dance with wolves is to turn away from the wonderful freedom available in Christ Jesus and "turn one's back on the sacred command" (v. 21). It is to imitate the crude behaviors of two animals considered unclean under Jewish law: dogs and pigs. Peter vividly portrays what it's like to return to a life of uncleanness. "Of them the proverbs are true: 'A dog returns to its vomit,' and, 'A sow that is washed goes back to her wallowing in the mud'" (v. 22).

Cults try to make you view your Christian faith as a box that walls you in. They hint, "You need to get beyond the Bible and find the real truth," or "Well, the Bible is OK as far as it goes, but our group's special guru (prophet, apostle, leader) gave us something else!"

But our Christian faith isn't a confining box; it's more like a mountaintop. And when you're standing with Christ on top of a mountain, to abandon him in any direction is to go downhill.

NOTES: CHAPTER ELEVEN

1. The second chapter of 2 Peter contains a number of parallels to the book of Jude, which describes many of the same characteristics of false teachers.

2. Ronald Enroth, *Churches That Abuse* (Grand Rapids: Zondervan, 1992), p. 103.

3. David Johnson and Jeff Van Vonderen, *The Subtle Power of Spiritual Abuse* (Minneapolis: Bethany House, 1991), p. 126.

4. Enroth, p. 103.

5. James Dobson, Focus on the Family Newsletter, February, 1993, p. 1.

CHAPTER TWELVE

A Great Day Coming

2 Peter 3:1-13

T here's a great day coming. I'm not talking about your birthday, graduation day, wedding day, or baseball's Opening Day. I'm not talking about payday, a day off from work, or even Christmas Day. There's a great day coming that makes any other special day pale by comparison. In fact, it's going to be such an eventful day, sometimes Scripture simply refers to it as "the day" or "that day" (Matthew 7:22; 1 Corinthians 3:13). I'm talking about the day when Jesus Christ returns to earth—the Day of Judgment.

Many times when I was a child, I waited excitedly for someone to come home. For example, I looked forward to my parents' return from the grocery store. Since we lived on a farm, grocery shopping was done during a weekly trip to town, and I liked it when my parents would return with a carload of fresh food. Even more, I looked forward to the excitement of waking up on Christmas morning to eat a delicious breakfast and open gifts. Do you remember the feeling?

But there's something far more important to anticipate. I wonder— how often do Christians really consider what we're saying when we mouth the words "Jesus is coming back"? Do we really believe this— not merely as a religious dogma, but as a cherished fact? How often do we even think about it nowadays? Does our expectation of Christ's return genuinely affect the way we live? Too often, I suspect, the return of Christ is something believers affirm as true but seldom consider as we go about our daily lives.

Recently I saw a Christian wearing a T-shirt that bore a large picture of the earth along with the clever message "Just Visiting!" It's so easy to get wrapped up in earthly things and forget that we are strangers on earth. Do we live each day in the awareness that we're aliens, "just visiting" on our way to Heaven?

How long has it been since you looked at the sky with childlike faith and realized that one of these days Jesus Christ is going to appear in the sky with power and glory and come to take us home? How long has it been since you prayed, as the apostle John did in the closing words of the Bible, "Come, Lord Jesus"?

The first-century Christians thought about this a lot. They even greeted each other with the Aramaic expression, *Marana tha,* which means "Come, O Lord" (1 Corinthians 16:22). Now, I'm quite sure the Lord doesn't want us to go around setting dates for his return, quitting our jobs, and wearing signs on our backs that proclaim "Repent, for the End Is Near!" But sometimes I wonder if we haven't become so turned off by end-time sensationalists that we have somehow lost the thrilling, wonderful realization that someday we will see our Lord face to face! The New Testament abounds with expectation about our "blessed hope—the glorious appearing of our great God and Savior, Jesus Christ" (Titus 2:13).

And the writings of Peter are no exception. In his first epistle, Peter encouraged his readers to look forward to the time "when Jesus Christ is revealed" (1:5-7, 13). He wrote about the day God "visits us" (2:12). He urged Christians to persevere when their faith was under fire, for "the end of all things is near" (4:7). He exhorted the church's elders to be faithful because "when the Chief Shepherd appears, you will receive the crown of glory that will never fade away" (5:4).

But by the time Peter wrote his second epistle, the church faced an increasing level of skepticism from influential people who evidently were denying that the Lord will return.

So in 2 Peter 3:1-13, Peter assures his readers that even though Christ's return may be delayed, it will eventually take place and we'd better be ready.

THE SCOFFERS' RIDICULE

Peter begins this section by stating his purpose for writing both of his letters: "Dear friends, this is now my second letter to you. I have written both of them as reminders to stimulate you to wholesome thinking" (v. 1). After his stormy denunciation of false teachers in the previous chapter, it's refreshing to find Peter returning to the warmer, more pastoral tone that usually characterizes his writing. He calls his readers "dear friends," or "beloved" (Greek *agapetoi)* three times in 2 Peter 3 (vv. 1, 8, 17). He wants his readers "to recall the words spoken in the past by the holy prophets" (that is, the ones who proclaimed God's Word during Old Testament times) and "the command given by our Lord and Savior through your apostles" (the ones who proclaimed God's Word during New Testament times). These verses not only remind us about the importance of memorizing Scripture ("recall the words"); they also point to the internal harmony of the Bible—both Old and New Testaments fit together and have value for the Christian.

A SKEPTICAL ATTITUDE

Some people have forgotten this, however. Peter warns, "you must understand that in the last days scoffers will come" (v. 3). The word translated "scoffers" is from a Greek verb (*empaizo)* which meant to ridicule, mock, or make fun of something. The same word appears in Matthew 27:29-31, where it describes the way the soldiers mocked Jesus before crucifying him. It's also used in Matthew 2:16 for the way the wise men or magi "tricked" or "outwitted" King Herod by returning to their country by a different route. The word conveys sort of a nose-thumbing attitude of mockery or disrespect. Peter warns that unbelievers will belittle the Christian faith. Evidently the idea of Christ's second coming will be a special target of their mockery. Peter wants his readers' faith to stand up under the fire of increasing skepticism.

Notice that the scoffers follow "their own evil desires" (v. 3). The kind of skepticism Peter warns about is not the sincere questioning of a struggling believer. Godly people sometimes struggle with legitimate questions and honest doubts. The Bible doesn't condemn that kind of searching; in fact, God specifically promises to reward the person who sincerely seeks the truth (Hebrews 11:6). On the other hand, a skeptical attitude can also be a sign of a sinful heart. The scoffers mentioned in this chapter were motivated by evil desires.

Often people who belittle what Christians believe do so, not for intellectual reasons, but for lifestyle reasons. Caught up in sinful habits they do not want to give up, the scoffers find it more convenient to mock the truth than to repent and live according to the truth. Such mockery springs more from arrogant pride than from genuine doubt. It's not always so, but sometimes intellectual objections against Christianity are simply a smoke screen for sin. In such cases, no amount of arguments will persuade the scoffer until he honestly acknowledges his wrongdoing and repents.

A MISTAKEN ASSUMPTION

The scoffers make a big mistake when they say, "Where is this 'coming' he promised? Ever since our fathers died, everything goes on as it has since the beginning of creation" (v. 4). They mistakenly assume that things on earth have always been the same as they are now, and that everything will always continue basically the same way.

Unfortunately, this point of view is quite common today. Accepting the presuppositions of naturalism, many people assume that miracles like the ones described in the Bible never actually happened, and that a future event like Christ's Second Coming will not happen either. There's also a scientific principle known as "uniformitarianism." This common sense concept just describes the way scientific laws function "uniformly" or consistently; in other words, we can count on nature to behave basically the same from day to day and century to century. In general, this principle is true, of course. Indeed, it's a testimony to the power and faithfulness of our creator, for God is the one who designed our natural laws and who uses them consistently to sustain our lives (Genesis 8:22; Psalm 148:1-6). Natural laws must not be viewed, though, as absolute and inviolable, for the same God who created them can also set them aside.

According to the Bible, it's simply not true to say that everything has always been the same and that nothing in nature will ever change. Don't forget, there's a great day coming!

AN OVERLOOKED LESSON

Instead of spending their time attacking Christians, the scoffers should have been studying world history! According to Peter, they have forgotten two important historical facts: creation and the flood. "But they deliberately forget that long ago by God's word the Heavens existed and the earth was formed out of water and by water. By these waters also the world of that time was deluged and destroyed" (vv. 5, 6).

Peter's thought-provoking words, written nearly two thousand years ago, still identify two key areas of concern for modern believers. Today the biblical doctrine of creation continues to come under attack from skeptics who choose to believe that the universe was produced by impersonal chance rather than by a personal creator. Further, many modern skeptics openly ridicule the idea that an ancient flood in Noah's day completely deluged and destroyed the world.

But Scripture insists that it was in fact "by God's word" that creation happened. And it was "by God's word" that the flood happened. There is compelling evidence in the realm of science that points to the reasonableness of these biblical truths.[1] And Peter warns, "By the same word the present Heavens and earth are reserved for fire, being kept for the day of judgment and destruction of ungodly men" (v. 7). The same Bible that tells about the creation and the flood that happened in the past, also foretells the future final destruction of the earth by fire.

Anyone who scoffs and tries to mock God should remember: ultimately, God will have the last word. "Do not be deceived: God cannot be mocked. A man reaps what he sows. The one who sows to please his sinful nature, from that sinful nature will reap destruction; the one who sows to please the Spirit, from the Spirit will reap eternal life" (Galatians 6:7).

These are solemn, disturbing words. But lest we become disheartened, Peter goes on to offer a message of hope and encouragement about the great day that is coming.

THE LORD'S REASSURANCE

"But do not forget this one thing, dear friends: With the Lord a day is like a thousand years, and a thousand years are like a day" (v. 8). As Peter does so often in his letters, here he alludes to a section of the Old Testament. Psalm 90 (the only psalm attributed to Moses) is a prayer that includes three important insights about time management: (1) *an expression of praise for God's eternality*—"For a thousand years in your sight are like a day that has just gone by, or like a watch in the night"; (2) *an observation about human mortality*—"The length of our days is seventy years—or eighty, if we have the strength; yet their span is but trouble and sorrow, for they quickly pass, and we fly away"; and (3) *a request for God's help in using our time wisely*—"Teach us to number our days aright, that we may gain a heart of wisdom" (Psalm 90:4, 10, 12).

GOD'S TIMELESSNESS

God sees time differently from the way we do. What we consider a long time is really a short time from God's eternal perspective. He is not limited by time or space. But our human perspective is very different. We tend to evaluate the passing of time based on the relative enjoyment or lack of enjoyment we're experiencing. When you're enjoying a relaxing vacation, talking with a fun-loving friend, or completing a satisfying project, time not only flies—it zooms by rapidly on supersonic wings. But when you're enduring a boring business meeting, driving along an uninteresting section of interstate highway, or sitting in the dentist's chair, time drags like a bad movie played at slow speed on your VCR.

We must learn to see time more from the Lord's perspective. Instead of evaluating the passing of time from the standpoint of *pleasure* (that is, by how much we're enjoying the moment), God seems to evaluate time from the standpoint of *purpose* (that is, by the way his perfect will is being fulfilled). For us, time can appear to be a trap; for God, it's a tool. For us, it's hard to remember the past and foresee the future; God always sees the big picture. While we pray, "Come, Lord Jesus," we must remember that the return of Christ is something "God will bring about in his own time" (1 Timothy 6:15).

What do we understand about such timelessness and patience? I get impatient because my computer is too slow—though it can still do a large amount of work in a fraction of the time required by old-fashioned typewriters. I feel irritated if I find myself having to use an old-fashioned rotary phone instead of today's push button variety—even though with a rotary phone, communication is swift and powerful compared to what past generations knew. I complain when traffic slows me down on the way to work—not thinking how slow travel was throughout most of human history as people rode horses or simply walked. I chafe when I'm forced to wait in a long line at a fast-food restaurant—forgetting how people in past generations (and in Third World nations yet today) often struggled simply to have enough food to eat at all. I struggle to fathom the patient perspective of a God who sees a thousand years as if they were merely a day.

Consider, too, the flip side of the coin: "With the Lord a day is like a thousand years." That is, one short day can be so eventful that, from God's perspective, it contains a thousand years' worth of significance. Consider, for example, the long-lasting impact of the day Adam and Eve sinned; or the day God gave the Ten Commandments to Moses; or the day Jesus Christ was born; or the most significant day of all, the day Jesus died on the cross.

God can pack a millennium of meaning into a moment of time.

GOD'S FAITHFULNESS

"The Lord is not slow in keeping his promise, as some understand slowness. He is patient with you" (v. 9). Sometimes we seem to "understand slowness" from a very immature perspective. When my daughter Michelle was small, we often played catch. She'd ask, "Dad, when can we play ball?" I'd answer, "At 4:30," then continue working on my project. By 4:15, Michelle would be tugging on my pant leg saying, "C'mon, Dad, you promised we could play ball." I'd say, "It's not time yet, honey." She'd be back again at 4:20, and again at 4:25. But you can be sure, by 4:30 sharp I'd pull on my sneakers, grab my ball glove, and jog out to the backyard. My actions may have seemed slow to Michelle, but there was no way I'd break a promise to my girl!

We need to see things from our heavenly Father's point of view. If it seems God's timing is slow, he isn't being cruel; he's being kind! He isn't being mean; he's being merciful! He isn't procrastinating; he's being "patient with you, not wanting anyone to perish, but everyone to come to repentance" (v. 9). If God seems to be delaying Jesus' second coming, it's simply so that lost people will have more time to repent of sin and turn to him.

My friend Leo Kuhn has served as the preacher at my home church for the last twenty-two years. Leo became a Christian and committed himself to ministry later in life. He says 2 Peter 3:9 is his favorite verse in the whole Bible! People like Leo are glad God was patient enough to allow them time to turn to him in faith.

The Lord takes no pleasure in seeing people perish (Ezekiel 18:32; 1 Timothy 2:4). As the *King James Version* translates this verse, God is "long-suffering" toward us. Though our suffering may seem long at times, God has suffered longer. It's hard to imagine his pain as he's waited for his prodigal children to come home.

Like a thundercloud rumbling in the distance, though, Peter warns us not to take advantage of God's patience. "But the day of the Lord will come like a thief. The Heavens will disappear with a roar; the elements will be destroyed by fire, and the earth and everything in it will be laid bare" (v. 10).

There's a great day coming—but it won't be a pleasant day for anyone who is outside of the saving grace of Jesus. In John's vision recorded in the book of Revelation, he saw a sobering time when "the kings of the earth, the princes, the generals, the rich, the mighty, and every slave and every free man hid in caves and among the rocks of the mountains. They called to the mountains and the rocks, 'Fall on us and hide us from the face of him who sits on the throne and from the wrath of the Lamb! For the great day of their wrath has come, and who can stand?'" (Revelation 6:15-17). God's gentle patience will someday give way to his final justice. The day will come swiftly ("like a thief"), noisily ("with a roar"), powerfully ("the elements will be destroyed by fire"), and decisively ("the earth and everything in it will be laid bare").

THE CHRISTIAN'S RESPONSIBILITY

With characteristic bluntness, Peter asks, "Since everything will be destroyed in this way, what kind of people ought you to be?" If this question were not so serious, it could almost sound like Peter was joking. The answer is so obvious, it's almost humorous.

What kind of people should we be? If my money is going to be destroyed someday along with the rest of the earth, does it make any sense to live solely for money? If my house, my clothes, my car, and all my other possessions are going to perish someday, how foolish I would be to focus my life's goals on them. "What kind of people ought you to be?" Serious Christians, that's what!

In his book *Disciples Are Made, Not Born*, Walter Henrichsen tells about a time during his college years when he was searching for a purpose in life. An engineering major, he was planning to become a civil engineer and build bridges, roads, and dams. That is—until he came across 2 Peter 3:10. He was shocked to realize that everything he planned to build would one day be destroyed. He reasoned, "Why give all my time and effort to build something which God had already said that He will burn?" In time, he determined that there are only two things that are worth devoting your whole life to: "In setting my life's objectives, I could give myself to *people* and the *Word of God*, and know that God was not going to follow me and burn them up."[2]

Henrichsen is quick to add, "This doesn't mean a person should not be a teacher, housewife, businessman, or even build bridges. To be involved in such a vocation may be the perfect will of God for your life. But God forbid that you should give your life in exchange for it!"[3]

God calls us to live holy and godly lives in the present as we look forward to the glorious future he has in store for us.

HOLY AND GODLY LIVES IN THE PRESENT

When Peter asks, "What kind of people ought you to be?," the word translated "what kind" (Greek *potapos*) literally meant something like, "of what country"—as if whatever is being described is foreign to our experiences or "out of this world."

It's the word used in 1 John 3:1 when the apostle John writes, "How great *(potapos)* is the love the Father has lavished on us, that we should be called children of God!" Bible teacher Knofel Staton writes that the word "stresses breath-taking amazement, astonishment, admiration, and excitement." According to Staton:

> When the winds obeyed Jesus, people asked, "What kind *(potapos)* of man is this that even the winds and the sea obey Him?" (Matthew 8:27). To say merely "kind" is too weak. They were saying, "What an astonishing, fantastic, amazing person this is. He's so great that we have nothing compared to Him in our culture. He's foreign to us." It was the same word Mary used to describe the angel's greeting to her—"what kind of salutation," fantastically marvelous (Luke 1:29). . . . We are to be a *potapos* people—fantastically, amazingly, astonishing people.[4]

Todd and Tami Carter are *potapos* people with astonishing faith. As newlyweds they served a term as missionaries in Africa. When they arrived in Tanzania, people asked them where they planned to live and set up their mission work. When they replied, "Masasi" (the name of a small village in the southeastern part of the country), people said, "Mwisho wa dunia!" Soon Todd and Tami discovered that *Mwisho wa dunia* is Swahili for "the end of the world." And as soon as they arrived in the village of Masasi, they learned why the Tanzanians called it that. The village was so remote it was hard even to find any fresh water to drink. Electricity was a rare luxury. The atmosphere was filled with the presence of evil—a witch doctor lived directly behind the Carters' house. The young missionaries struggled with bouts of malaria, and the nearest medical facility was thirty miles away. It really felt like they had come to "the end of the world."

But, of course, Jesus said his people would take his Word to the uttermost parts of the earth. And Todd and Tami say, "Strangely enough, we found ourselves experiencing peace and joy there in that remote village. It took going to 'the end of the world' for us to understand what it means to truly lean on Jesus." Their faith stood up under fire.

LOOKING FORWARD TO THE FUTURE

There's a great day coming, and we can "look forward to the day of God and speed its coming" (v. 12). How can we "speed the coming" of the end? The Greek word translated "speed" (*speudo*) could mean "to hasten" or "cause to happen quickly." Many Christians believe that we hasten the day of God through *evangelism* (based on Matthew 24:14—"And this gospel of the kingdom will be preached in the whole world as a testimony to all nations, and then the end will come"), through *prayer* (as in the Lord's Prayer recorded in Matthew 6:10, "Your kingdom come, your will be done on earth as it is in Heaven"), or through *repentance and obedience to the Lord* (suggested perhaps by Acts 3:19-21). If any of these understandings is correct, it certainly makes us pause to think that in some way known only to God, the actions of God's faithful here on earth are involved in his determination of the end of time.

The word *speudo* can also mean being "zealous," or "industrious," or "to greatly desire" something. Thus, the *American Standard Version* of the Bible translates 2 Peter 3:12, "looking for and earnestly desiring the coming of the day of God." If this interpretation is correct, Peter's emphasis in 2 Peter 3:12 is more on the fact that it's our hearts' desire to see the day of God come quickly—not that we do something to make it come more speedily.

We certainly have a lot to look forward to: "in keeping with his promise we are looking forward to a new Heaven and a new earth, the home of righteousness" (v. 13).

There's a great day coming. More than that, there's a great Savior coming. "For the Lord himself will come down from Heaven, with a loud command, with the voice of the archangel and with the trumpet call of God, and the dead in Christ will rise first. After that, we who are still alive and are left will be caught up together with them in the clouds to meet the Lord in the air. And so we will be with the Lord forever. Therefore encourage each other with these words" (1 Thessalonians 4:16-18). Before he returns and time is no more, he invites us to come to him in faith.

NOTES ON CHAPTER TWELVE

1. See Walt Brown, *In the Beginning: Compelling Evidence for Creation and the Flood* (Phoenix, AZ: Center for Scientific Creation, 1995).

2. Walter A. Henrichsen, *Disciples Are Made, Not Born* (Wheaton, IL: Victor Books, 1974), pp. 152-154.

3. Ibid., p. 155.

4. Knofel Staton, *Thirteen Lessons on First, Second, and Third John* (Joplin: College Press, 1980), p. 55.

CHAPTER THIRTEEN

Don't Burn Out—
Burn On!

2 Peter 3:14-18

When I was a boy, I hoped to grow tall enough to be a star basketball player. My goals were to be at least six feet five inches tall and to play in arenas packed with thousands of cheering fans. Unfortunately, my genes didn't cooperate, and I had to settle for five feet eleven inches and an occasional game of hoops in the driveway.

Growth doesn't always mean achieving the goals you set for yourself. Sometimes we grow most by accepting the changes and unexpected opportunities God brings our way. My life has taken quite a few unexpected twists and turns, and each one has helped me to grow. I was born and raised on a farm in Ohio, but I ended up spending ten years as a minister in New York. I always assumed I would marry someday, but I never could have predicted that I'd marry a woman whose maiden name (Faust) was identical to my own last name. I expected to be a dad, but years ago I wouldn't have predicted that I'd adopt a child from Korea. Just as I settled into my teaching career after eight years as a Bible college professor, I accepted an invitation to become editor of *The Lookout* magazine and found myself growing yet again—struggling to adapt to a whole new world of deadlines, computer graphics, and journalistic jargon.

Now firmly entrenched in middle age—halfway between Generation X and Generation X-ray—I've found that it's often easier to talk about growth than it is to really grow! It's tempting to stop doing the things that lead to growth. We become stagnant. Stuck in a rut. Bored with

ourselves and boring to others. Afraid to risk, to change, to try anything new. If we refuse to grow, we don't experience abundant life, but
a slow death. We burn out. Whenever spiritual inertia replaces spiritual
energy, we settle for far less than the challenging, stretching life Christ
intended for his disciples.

It can happen to whole churches as well as individuals. We pine
after the "good old days" instead of figuring out how to make the coming days better. It's easier to gripe than it is to grow; easier to be petty
than to be purposeful. We allow our business meetings to degenerate
into long-winded discussions of bureaucratic minutiae instead of
power-filled moments of prayer for God's guidance. Apathetic and
uncommitted, we act as if our theme song is "I Shall Not Be Moved."
We become *in*ward-focused, *in*flexible, and *in*dividualistic, then wonder why we're *in* trouble! For many churches today, enough time and
energy already have been spent maintaining the status quo. It's time to
move out, move ahead, and move on.

We become like road-weary travelers who've spent too many hours
in the car. We need to stop and stretch our limbs. Get out and walk a
while. Take in the scenery. Review the road map once again to remind
us where we're headed. Then get back in the car and get going again.

Never stop growing. Keep fanning the flames of faith. This was
Peter's last message to the Christians he loved so much. Peter himself
continued to grow in his walk with Christ. When he wrote 2 Peter near
the end of his life, he was still serving, still growing, still finding a way
to be useful in God's kingdom. The closing verses at the end of 2 Peter
seem especially powerful when we remember that these are the last
recorded words of the great apostle—sort of his "last will and testament" expressing his desires and intentions to be carried out after his
death. "But grow in the grace and knowledge of our Lord and Savior
Jesus Christ. To him be glory both now and forever! Amen" (v. 18).

FANNING NEW FLAMES

One morning a couple of years ago, I woke up to the familiar sound
of the 6:00 news broadcast over the clock radio next to my bed. The

news that day was particularly depressing. A woman had shot her boyfriend. A man admitted poisoning his wife. Political campaigns were growing more negative and bitter. Even Jim Scott, the usually upbeat radio deejay, commented on how bad the news sounded that day. Then he said, "There's got to be something good going on this morning! Won't somebody call in with some *good* news?"

As I lay there in bed, still half asleep, I thought, "What an opportunity! Some Christian needs to call in. That's a 50,000-watt station that can be heard in thirty-eight states. Somebody needs to take advantage of this chance to say something positive for Christ!"

Then through my sleeping daze, it struck me: *I am somebody.* Pulling my bathrobe around me, I dialed the phone number for the radio station. And a few minutes later, Jim Scott put me on the air with the words, "Dave Faust, tell us some *good news!*"

Thinking quickly, I told how my church had recently purchased an old church building in the center-city neighborhood of Clifton Heights. It was easy for me to share my excitement as I told how university students and community residents were pooling their resources and working hard to refurbish an old building to use as a place of worship, an activity center for youth, a coffee house, and other purposes. After a few minutes, the deejay thanked me for calling, and I hung up the phone. I looked at myself—still standing there half-asleep in my bathrobe—and laughed out loud as I thought, "I must be dreaming! I'm barely awake enough to remember my name, and I think I just spoke on the radio to hundreds of thousands of people!"

My sleepy-eyed daughter Michelle opened the door to my bedroom, and as she rubbed her eyes, she said with bewilderment, "Dad, did I just hear you on the radio?" I felt like I was dreaming. But actually I was growing! Without even searching for it, I had stumbled onto another surprising, unexpected way to share God's good news.

Peter's life took many unexpected twists and turns after he became a disciple of Jesus and started spreading the good news of Christ. He started out as a humble fisherman. He expected to sail the Sea of Galilee, but not to walk on it (Matthew 14:29). Peter never seemed to lack for something to say, but it's doubtful he could have imagined that before his life was over, he would preach boldly before his nation's supreme court, the Sanhedrin (Acts 5:27-42). Peter was quick to brag about his loyalty to Jesus, but then he learned the hard way about his own fallibility a few hours later when he denied the Lord three times (Matthew 26:31-35, 69-75). When the Lord's angel arrived to rescue him from prison, Peter thought he was dreaming (Acts 12:9). The Lord just kept bringing new adventures and growth-producing experiences into Peter's life.

He had probably expected to stay anchored close to his native Galilee. But it appears that he ended up traveling extensively for the sake of the gospel (1 Corinthians 9:5; 1 Peter 5:13). Almost despite himself, Peter never stopped growing.

One of the biggest surprises of Peter's life probably came on the day when the Spirit of God commanded him to go to the house of a Gentile soldier, a centurion named Cornelius.

KOSHER AND ITALIAN DON'T MIX

On second thought, it shouldn't have been that big a surprise. Peter already knew about Jesus' love for non-Jewish people. One of Jesus' first public sermons, delivered in the Lord's hometown synagogue in Nazareth, included references to God's kindness to a non-Jewish widow and to Naaman the Syrian in the days of Elisha (Luke 4:24-27). Peter was surely aware that Jesus had shown kindness to a Greek woman from Syrian Phoenicia by freeing her daughter from demon possession (Mark 7:24-30). And he no doubt knew that the Lord had revealed himself as the Messiah to a Samaritan woman (John 4:25, 26). If he was listening carefully, he could have caught the inference of Jesus' words, "I have other sheep that are not of this sheep pen. I must bring them also. They too will listen to my voice, and there shall be one flock and one shepherd" (John 10:16). Surely Peter knew about the wide-ranging curiosity about Christ—magi from the east who came to visit when Jesus was young (Matthew 2:1-12), Greeks who came to the Jewish Passover and requested, "Sir, we would like to see Jesus" (John 12:21), and even a battle-hardened Roman centurion who cried out at the foot of the cross, "Surely this man was the Son of God!"

(Mark 15:39). Peter should have known that Jesus was interested in saving people of all races and nations. The promise of John 3:16 isn't limited to Galileans, or Jews, or Americans; "God so loved the world." And Jesus' instructions to Peter and the other apostles in Acts 1:8 clearly spelled out the worldwide scope of Christian mission: "You will be my witnesses in Jerusalem, and in all Judea and Samaria, and to the ends of the earth."

But some lessons are hard to learn. Some growth steps are hard to take. And racial prejudice seems to be one of the toughest personal weaknesses to overcome.

I remember driving past a billboard one time when my daughter Mindy was just learning to read. The billboard showed the faces of a group of children representing different ethnic groups, accompanied by a sign that read, "Stop Racism."

Mindy looked at the sign, then asked innocently, "Mom and Dad?"

"Yes, honey?"

Drawing out each syllable as she struggled to pronounce this unfamiliar word, she said, "What's *rack-i-sim*?"

In her childlike naiveté, Mindy didn't even know how to pronounce "racism." Even less did she understand the wicked concept that people would judge others by the color of their skin or the nation of their origin.

Peter's biases were deeply ingrained, instilled by a proud Jewish culture that, by his lifetime, already reached back through many centuries to great Hebrew heroes like Abraham and Moses. By Peter's day, long-held Jewish hatred for Gentiles was further reinforced by the fact that the Roman Empire ruled Palestine, and Roman soldiers were intruders, occupying by force what the Jews saw as God's promised land. Peter's feelings about preaching to Gentiles were probably a lot like Jonah's feelings long before about preaching in Nineveh, the national capital of the Assyrian enemy.

Imagine Peter's state of mind as he arrived at Cornelius's house. The eager voices inside didn't sound like Peter's usual Jewish friends. Cornelius led a group of soldiers known as the Italian Regiment (Acts 10:1). There was a European accent to the conversation. No doubt the house was decorated differently from Peter's home back in Galilee. Even the food smelled different—more like pasta and garlic than bagels and matzo balls! Even though he was convinced God had sent him to Cornelius's house, Peter's instincts recoiled at this new and uncomfortable experience.

GOD DOESN'T PLAY FAVORITES

Surely Peter was touched, though, by Cornelius's humble greeting. It wasn't common for a rugged centurion to fall at his feet in reverence before another man. Peter quickly made him get up. "Stand up," he said, "I am only a man myself" (Acts 10:26). And Peter openly admitted his feelings of awkwardness about the whole situation, explaining, "You are well aware that it is against our law for a Jew to associate with a Gentile or visit him" (Acts 10:28).

Yet, the more Peter conversed with Cornelius, the more his lingering reservations about all this melted away. (Come to think of it, there's probably no better remedy for prejudice than direct communication like this—in someone's home, face to face and heart to heart.) Listen to Peter's conclusions: "God has shown me that I should not call any man impure or unclean" (Acts 10:28). "I now realize how true it is that God does not show favoritism but accepts men from every nation who fear him and do what is right" (Acts 10:34, 35). "Jesus Christ . . . is Lord of all" (Acts 10:36). Incredible statements coming from someone like Peter who in the past had no use for Gentiles!

Now, lest we conclude all this was an immediate, easy change for Peter, we need to recall that years later he still struggled with his attitude toward Gentiles. One time, when Peter visited the new Christians in Antioch, he separated himself from the Gentile believers because he feared the criticisms of the Jewish believers there. So great was his hypocrisy that the apostle Paul showed Peter his error and "opposed him to his face . . . in front of them all" in a biblical confrontation of epic proportions (Galatians 2:11-14)!

It's hard to outgrow old behavior patterns that tie us to sinful attitudes we developed in the past. It wasn't easy for Peter. But eventually he did learn to accept Gentiles fully as his brothers and sisters in

Christ. "Once you were not a people," Peter wrote to churches comprised of folk from different ethnic backgrounds, "but now you are the people of God; once you had not received mercy, but now you have received mercy" (1 Peter 2:10).

Like Peter, we need to keep growing and fanning new flames of faith. Don't burn out—burn on!

FUELING THE FIRE

In a sense, the whole book of 2 Peter can be summed up in the little exhortation, "Know more, and grow more." But in practical terms, what does it mean to grow in grace and knowledge? What kind of fuel can keep the fire of faith burning brightly?

GROWTH TAKES EFFORT

"So then, dear friends, since you are looking forward to this, make every effort to be found spotless, blameless and at peace with him" (2 Peter 3:14). As people who look forward to the return of Christ, it's only fitting that we should make every effort to grow in holiness and Christlikeness.

I remember seeing a newspaper advertisement for a little battery-operated gadget touted as a "European body shaper." The ad claimed that you could tone up your muscles without effort as the device sent tiny electrical impulses through wires attached to your body. With unbridled enthusiasm, bold promises jumped off the page in big red letters: you can enjoy the benefits of "three thousand sit-ups without moving an inch;" "ten miles of jogging lying flat on your back;" "just fifteen minutes a day replaces countless hours of body-racking exercise as it spot-tones your entire figure . . . all while you watch TV, read a book, or simply snooze and relax!" Buyer, beware. A no-effort approach to physical fitness won't bring the results you desire; nor will a no-effort approach to spiritual fitness.

We are saved by God's grace, not through our human efforts. Nevertheless, Christ calls us to obedience and discipleship.

When I was seventeen, I spent a summer working for a skilled carpenter. He asked me, "Are you interested in this just as a summer job? Or do you want to be an apprentice?" What he meant was, "Are you here just to make some money, or do you really want to become a master carpenter like I am?" I had to be honest—I wanted only a summer job. I didn't have enough interest to become an apprentice. I didn't want to put in the extra time and receive the extra training. I just wanted to do the basics, collect my paycheck, and go home.

Christ calls us to discipleship. One Greek lexicon lists "apprentice" as one of the possible translations for the Greek word for disciple, *mathetes*.[1] We need to walk so closely with Jesus, our master carpenter, that we learn everything we possibly can from him. Discipleship requires far more than a "Christmas and Easter only" or even a "Sunday only" kind of commitment. It means denying ourselves, taking up our crosses daily, and following Christ (Luke 9:23, 24). It means making the effort to identify other more mature believers who can be our spiritual mentors, like Paul was to Timothy and Titus, and it means finding younger believers like Timothy and Titus whom we can encourage and nurture in the faith. Helping others grow is worth the effort. It's one of the best ways to keep growing ourselves.

GROWTH TAKES STUDY

Peter points back to "our dear brother Paul" who "also wrote you with the wisdom that God gave him" (v. 15). Notice, Peter wouldn't have called Paul his dear brother if had held a grudge for the rebuke Paul gave him in Antioch (Galatians 2:11-14), or if he were jealous and suspicious of Paul's work as some people were (see Philippians 1:15-18). These great men saw themselves as coworkers, not competitors—an important lesson for church leaders who privately struggle with the temptation to be competitive and jealous toward other ministers. Peter and Paul recognized that they were on the same team!

Some of Paul's writings, Peter notes, "contain some things that are hard to understand" (2 Peter 3:16). Many a Bible student will say "Amen" to that—especially if you've ever puzzled over one of Paul's long, in-depth sentences in a letter like Romans. Notice, though, Peter doesn't say these words of Scripture are *impossible* to understand, just that they're hard, or difficult. Scripture is like a beautiful ocean beach: you can enjoy the view as you walk along the shore, but you can also enjoy an exhilarating dive into the depths. The Bible is simple enough that a child can understand its basic message, but complex enough to challenge the most brilliant scholar.

Peter shows tremendous respect for Paul's writings. He says Paul wrote with God-given wisdom; he links Paul's letters with "the other Scriptures" (thus acknowledging their inspiration and canonicity); and he warns that when "ignorant and unstable people distort" these or any other Scriptures, they do so "to their own destruction" (vv. 15, 16).

Spiritual growth requires careful study of the Word. How else can you grow in knowledge of the Lord and his will? How else can you "be on your guard so you may not be carried away by the error of lawless men and fall from your secure position" (v. 17)?

GROWTH TAKES GOD'S HELP

But spiritual growth isn't merely about accumulating more and more "head-knowledge." Peter calls us to "grow in grace" too. For many of us, the phrase "grow in knowledge" is easier to understand than the phrase, "grow in grace." In practical terms, perhaps grace-growth could be measured by asking ourselves questions like these:

• Am I more gracious and merciful toward others than I used to be?
• Do I understand more about God's grace than I used to know?
• Am I growing in my appreciation for the depth of God's mercy and love?
• Am I employing the gifts God has graciously supplied?
• Are my acts of Christian service motivated by ever-increasing gratitude, or simply by a sense of grudging obligation?

God doesn't leave us to struggle on our own. One of the reasons he gives us the gift of his Holy Spirit is to help us keep growing. Far more than our own willpower is at work; the power of God is also at work as a believer grows in faith and holiness (Philippians 2:12, 13).

Peter's final words seem a fitting summation of the great apostle's life: "To him [Jesus Christ] be glory both now and forever! Amen" (v. 18). Many years before, it was a generous assessment to call Peter a "rock." Then he was a diamond in the rough. Jesus called him from the Galilean fishing docks to a life of adventure as a Christian leader. Jesus saw his potential, and now, after years of refinement, Peter was a valuable gem indeed—highly polished and shining brightly.

Peter never lost his heart's desire to point others toward the One who is more precious than silver or gold, more beautiful than diamonds. Despite his faults, and through all the refining fires, Peter's faith endured. And now, as this great man of God neared death, his goal was still to give glory to his Lord. Whatever else you think about Peter, always remember this: he simply loved Jesus.

Never stop growing. And when times get tough and your faith comes under fire, do what Peter did: simply love Jesus.

NOTES: CHAPTER THIRTEEN

1. F. Wilbur Gingrich, *Shorter Lexicon of the Greek New Testament* (Chicago: The University of Chicago Press, 1965), p. 129.